# HOW TO
# CHOOSE A
# YOUTH
# PASTOR

# HOW TO
# CHOOSE A
# YOUTH
# PASTOR

## Paul Borthwick

OLIVER
NELSON

THOMAS NELSON PUBLISHERS
*Nashville*

Published in Nashville, Tennessee, by Oliver-Nelson Books, a division of Thomas Nelson, Inc., Publishers, and distributed in Canada by Word Communications, Ltd., Richmond, British Columbia.

The Bible version used in this publication is THE NEW KING JAMES VERSION. Copyright © 1979, 1980, 1982, Thomas Nelson, Inc., Publishers.

The following publishers have given permission to use material from copyrighted works: From *The Youth Minister's Survival Guide* by Len Kageler. Copyright © 1992 by Youth Specialities. Used by permission of Zondervan Publishing House. From *Create in Me a Youth Ministry* by Ridge Burns and Pam Campbell, published by Victor Books, 1986, SP Publications, Inc., Wheaton, IL 60187.

Printed in the United States of America.

**Library of Congress Cataloging-in-Publication Data**

Borthwick, Paul, 1954–
How to choose a youth pastor / Paul Borthwick.
  p.  cm.
Includes bibliographical references.
ISBN 0-8407-9669-2
  1. Clergy—Appointment, call, and election.  2. Church work with youth.  I. Title.
BV664.B67  1993
254—dc20
                                    93-11007
                                      CIP

1 2 3 4 5 6 — 98 97 96 95 94 93

# Contents

# Acknowledgments

To present as much helpful information as possible to groups endeavoring to choose a youth pastor, I have tried to solicit the advice of youth ministry experts throughout the country to supplement the content of this book.

When I quote directly from a book, the text is noted. Where there are quotations without notes, however, I refer to personal correspondence or telephone calls.

I owe a special measure of thanks to Wayne Rice, Steve Macchia, Tom McLaughlin, Jimmy Dodd and the folks at Mitchell Road Presbyterian Church, Les Hughey, Donald Jones, Len Kageler, Paul Fleischmann, and Jim Tonkowich.

I also am deeply grateful for the help of my coworkers in the ministry here at Grace Chapel: Mike Allen, Jim Petipas, and Charles Smith.

And as always, I owe a special debt of gratitude to my precious wife, Christie, who allows me to cut into family time to pursue my avocation as an author.

# Introduction

Pastor Andrews made his point emphatically: "The growth of Westside Church has been a direct result of our effective youth ministry. Bill served effectively as a youth pastor, and now we need to find his replacement. The momentum of our church depends on the choices we make. We must find an effective youth minister."

The situation differs at First Baptist. The youth ministry has been growing without a lot of attention. Motivated students have been bringing their friends, but the group has now become too large to be led by volunteer adults and students. The church board has decided it's time to look for a youth ministry professional—a youth pastor—but past growth without such a leader causes some doubts to arise: Will a professional be able to build on the situation as it is now? Will a youth pastor be able to direct these volunteers and students?

Other churches face the decision of choosing a

youth pastor from other perspectives. One church needed a youth pastor who could help heal the hurts caused by the moral failure of the former youth leader. Another church desired someone who could help stem the tide of young people leaving the church; they needed someone who could make Christian faith relevant to their youths.

Whatever the perspective, churches and church boards face similar questions: Who is the best choice? What are we looking for in a youth minister? What do we have to offer? What are the needs of our youths and their families?

This book is for men and women who serve as pastors, Search Committee members, or directors in Christian education—any persons who are evaluating how to choose a youth pastor for their church. (Note: I will refer throughout the book to the people involved in the search process as the "Search Committee." This is not intended to exclude other churches or systems where the process may not be quite so formal.) The goal of the book is to stimulate searchers with the questions to ask to get the best possible "fit" of a youth leader with a church.

As a result, the book may not offer all the answers. Instead, it may stir more questions. But these questions, combined with practical advice, stories from other churches, and useful tools, can equip the Search Committee to make the wisest choice possible in selecting a youth leader who will, in turn, lead the church to greater effectiveness in ministry to young people.

## *The Basic Process: An Overview*

Throughout these pages, I try to cover the myriad of issues that a Search Committee will face in meeting the challenge of finding a compatible youth pastor.

The process, however, is fairly basic and can be summarized in five steps.[1]

**Step 1: Defining the task.** Before any candidate is considered, the Search Committee or the church leaders must answer certain questions (including, Who should serve on a Search Committee?). These definitional questions are addressed in Parts 1, 2, and 3.

**Step 2: Developing selection criteria.** Part 3 begins it, and Part 4 develops it so that the Search Committee can form an effective Youth Pastor Profile. This step includes evaluating resumes plus creating a list of qualities, experiences, and qualifications that describes the person the Search Committee thinks will best fit the church.

**Step 3: Evaluating the candidates.** Applications, screenings, and interviews are covered in Part 5.

This step includes using references as well as watching out for warning signs in the interviewing stages of the search.

**Step 4: Making the decision.** What is the best way to analyze all of the data accumulated and arrive at a final decision? How can Search Committee members agree? Part 6 addresses this "crossroads" phase of the process.

**Step 5: Implementing the decision.** Inviting the candidate does not mean that the Search Committee's work ends. An effective Search Committee gets involved in helping the new youth pastor and the youth ministry through the transition, the topic covered in Part 7.

The Appendixes conclude the book by offering some resources to assist Search Committees throughout the entire process, including sample questions, job descriptions, and people to ask for contacts.

## NOTE

1. These five steps are a modification of the six steps in effective hiring recommended by Pat MacMillan in *Hiring Excellence* (Colorado Springs: NavPress, 1992), p. 45.

# HOW TO
## CHOOSE A
# YOUTH
# PASTOR

## Part 1

# The Need

*Chapter 1*

# Does Our Church Need a Youth Pastor?

◆

Imagine yourself as a church leader in the early 1970s. Many of the baby boomers (persons born between 1946 and 1964) are hitting adolescence full stride. The "revolutions"—sex, drugs, rock'n' roll, and even the Jesus Movement—of the 1960s have forced the church to look more seriously at the youth subculture and the corresponding needs. Stuart Briscoe awakened the church with his book *Where Was the Church When the Youth Exploded?*[1] and Larry Richards released his first edition of *Youth Ministry: Its Renewal in the Local Church.*[2]

In the early seventies, most churches anxiously entertained the notion of hiring a youth pastor—

3

either (positively) to reach out to the youths in the community or (negatively) to hang on to the youths in the church. Teenagers constituted one of the largest segments of society. A youth pastor was a natural priority for any church desiring to be relevant.

In the 1990s, the situation has become far more complicated. Needs of youths do not dominate the landscape of challenges facing the church as they once did. Ministry to senior adults, programs for single adults, and intervention with dysfunctional families all vie for the high priority attention once given to youth ministry.

That does not mean young people today are less needy. The breakdown of the family unit, increase in sexual activity, and volume of temptations facing teenagers have led to greater needs than ever before. The contemporary youth worker must be alert to issues like anorexia, abuse, AIDS, and the New Age Movement.

So does your church need a youth minister? If your church has young people on the rolls or is located in a community where young people ages ten to twenty exist, my instinctive response is YES! Young people of the nineties need the special love, instruction, and effort that a youth pastor can provide.

But your church governing board probably does not care what I think, so here are some key issues to consider when asking, Do we need a youth minister?

## *What Are Our Church's Priorities?*

Churches tend to take one of two outlooks at the world. One church sees itself as a fortress against a world of evil. The goal is to provide a safe haven for the Christian community. When the leaders of a "fortress" church think of youth ministry, they think of a program that will preserve the church's young people, protect them from the evils of the world, and provide programs offering a Christian alternative to worldly activities.

Another church takes an "advancement" perspective. Its members believe that Christians are Jesus' "salt" and "light" in the world (see Matt. 5); they are to permeate and penetrate the world in which they live. They understand the promise of Matthew 16:18—"the gates of Hades shall not prevail against it [the church]"—correctly. The church is on the attack, moving in on the gates of the kingdom of Satan to release and save those that he is holding captive, and the church will be the ultimate victor!

The Search Committee (and the church leaders) should sit down and ask, Do we see ourselves with a "fortress" mentality or an "advancement" mentality? In reality, a healthy church functions as both, but what is the *top* priority? Is most of the money spent on concerns within the church? Is the focus on mobilizing adults to do outreach—whether evangelism or ministries of mercy and compassion—in the community?

If the church's priority reflects that insular, fortress mentality, it will be very difficult to build a youth ministry that goes beyond maintaining programs with the aim of saving the church's young people from a corrupt world.

Donald Posterski, an expert with InterVarsity Christian Fellowship of Canada, asks questions along these lines that church leaders must wrestle with:

> Is the church a place where we call people to come and live their Christian life out within the confines of the institution, or does the church exist to equip people to go into the world and be the church? If our mentality is that we do ministry when we gather people inside the church, we're not going to be effective. Does the institution exist to serve, or to be served? Until we get that straight, until the energies of the church and the resources of youth workers are poured into people, we will have a shallow understanding of what it is to be a follower of Jesus Christ, and thus a shallow, ineffective ministry in our culture.[3]

A Search Committee must identify the top priority of the church because it inevitably trickles over into the expectations of the youth ministry.

## *What Are the Demographics of Our Church?*

Church researcher George Barna writes,

> In the mid-90's, the focus of growth [in education] will shift to the high schools. During the last five

years of the 90's, the enrollment in high schools will grow three times faster than that of elementary and junior high schools. Once again, there will be a substantial need for additional facilities and teachers to handle the Boomlet population.[4]

Therefore, there will also be a need for renewed and expanded church efforts to reach teens.

Barna continues,

Our surveys consistently show that more than two-thirds of all adults who have accepted Christ as their Savior made their decision to do so before the age of 18. Obviously, the best time to reach them with the gospel is while they are young and impressionable, during the period in which they are solidifying their values and key attitudes. Time is rapidly running out for us to reach today's children and adolescents. We will not have such a large number of youths to evangelize for many years to come.[5]

Quotations like these make us snap to attention. Obviously, we need a youth pastor! But before reacting, the Search Committee and fellow church leaders ought to check out the demographics of the community versus North America at large. Ask,

- How many upcoming children are there?
- How many existing youths?
- What type of families are moving to our area?
- Where are the unreached youths?

• If all of the young people are over age sixteen, what will the future of the youth ministry be?

## *What Are the Demographics of Our Region?*

This is a sister question to the previous one. The Search Committee should survey the schools in the region from which church families come and into which the church hopes to reach. How many of these communities have increasing numbers of children coming up?

In the mid-1980s, in response to a declining youth population, our town of Lexington, Massachusetts, began closing junior high buildings and making them into condominiums. The decline in the population of children, however, was reversing at grade two. The town was shortsighted and failed to plan for the future. Now those children are entering junior high school. The town is short on facilities and personnel.

In contrast, our church studied the demographics and decided to intensify our efforts with junior high ministry. In the early nineties, we began a process leading to the hiring of a full-time junior high pastor. The person was hired in 1992. At this writing, our junior high ministry averages thirty more students per week than our senior high ministry; the demographics of our region helped us see the handwriting on the wall.

Studying demographics can also help the Search Committee identify the types of ministry to students that the church can have in the region. In one community in the Pacific Northwest, the population is made up of a fifty-fifty split between the families of white-collar executives and lumber industry laborers. The respective cultures, socio-economic standings, and religious backgrounds (Lutheran versus Catholic) create two very different subcultures of teenagers at the local schools.

One church, concerned about reaching these youths, has looked at the demographics, and now it is asking if it can build one unified youth ministry or if it needs to identify the children of the two groups, reach them in different ways, and then try to incorporate them into a group that meets once per month.

Demographic studies help the Search Committee understand issues related to population growth or decline, ethnic differences within the church or community, and target groups of young people. With these understandings, the Search Committee can identify the type of youth pastor that the church will need.

## *What Are Some Existing Perceived Needs?*

Perhaps the Search Committee should ask, Why are we looking for a youth pastor?

- Has a beloved youth leader resigned and the Search Committee is looking for a replacement? If so, what kind of person will it take to replace that leader?

- Have there been a series of teen suicides (or other teen-related tragedies) in the community and the church is now trying to respond to the needs of hurting youths? Perhaps this will direct the Search Committee to look for someone skilled in counseling.
- Has a study shown that youths are graduating from high school and then leaving the church? Then perhaps the focus should shift to someone gifted as a pastor/discipler of youths—someone who can develop the leadership potential of existing teenagers in the church.

Any variety of perceived needs in the church or community can direct the focus of the Youth Pastor Search Committee. Unreached youths in neighboring schools may cry out for an evangelist. Inactive youths or the latchkey children of single-parent households may lead toward a search for someone to act as a youth social coordinator.

The Search Committee must decide the priorities related to these perceived needs. Understanding these needs enables the Search Committee to realize what strengths to look for as the search for the youth pastor begins.

## *What Does Our Pastor Think?*

In general, this rule stands: if the senior pastor has not agreed that a youth pastor is needed, the Search Committee may face a very rough road ahead. To ensure long-term success, the wise Search Committee will spend time at the outset trying to reach agreement with the senior pastor about not only the concept but also the type of youth pastor needed. (We will cover more on this in Part 2, especially regarding the senior pastor as a member of the Search Committee.)

The best church situation includes enthusiastic endorsement from the senior pastor about the need for a youth pastor. One youth pastor described his church setting where such endorsement occurred (and continues to occur): "The pastor welcomed me as his coworker, and we have become good friends. He loves and supports what I do. When asked, he gives insights and suggestions, but he gives me freedom to try almost anything. He considers me a true partner in ministry, although he himself is a very strong leader. We pray together every Wednesday. He believes in me and trusts me to use my gifts to carry out the youth ministry."

Who are the pastors most eager to create that kind of youth ministry environment? Which senior pastors are looking for a youth pastor? Usually, they

- have teenagers.
- have been leading the youth group single-handedly and sense their inadequacy.
- have experienced the powerful potential of youth ministry in their own lives.
- have a vision for reaching and discipling the youths of the church *and* the youths of the community.

## *Does Our Church Need a Youth Pastor?*

If you have purchased this book, chances are, you have already answered yes to this question, but church priorities, demographics, perceived needs, and the pastor's opinion all contribute to the Search Committee's answer. Now the question becomes, What type of youth pastor is needed? The following chapters help in discovering this answer.

### NOTES

1.  Stuart Briscoe, *Where Was the Church When the Youth Exploded?* (Grand Rapids: Zondervan, 1972).

2.  Larry Richards, *Youth Ministry: Its Renewal in the Local Church* (Grand Rapids: Zondervan, 1972).

3.  Donald Posterski, interviewed in *Youthworker,* Winter 1986, p. 62.

4.  George Barna, *The Frog in the Kettle* (Ventura, Calif.: Regal, 1990), p. 201.

5.  Barna, *The Frog,* p. 205.

# Part 2

# The Search Committee

## Chapter 2

# Who Is Doing the Searching?

I've had a number of conversations and received an abundance of correspondence concerning the search process. Allow me to paint several worst-case scenarios related to the search for a youth minister:

- The Search Committee is made up entirely of parents who disliked the previous youth leader and are now looking for a superhuman. After two years of looking, they all resign in frustration.
- In the search process, committee members get into furious arguments, and several of them resign from the committee; one family actually leaves the church.

- The Search Committee calls someone who reveals a few months after arriving that he really wants to move out of youth ministry and into a ministry to young adults.

- The Search Committee unanimously approves a candidate, but the teenagers totally reject the choice.

- The Search Committee is dominated by one out-spoken individual whose understanding of youth ministry arose out of his experiences in the 1950s.

- The Search Committee works for eight months to identify a candidate, and the pastor, elders, and/or ruling church board veto the recommendation because they have not felt that there was enough communication with other church leaders in the search process.

Although no church experiences *all* of these problems, similar scenarios are possible, especially if there has not been a careful amount of work done in selecting and preparing the Search Committee.

Thus, before we start identifying the ideal fit of youth pastor and church, we need to decide how to maximize choices of the team of people to look for the prospective youth pastor. The book of Proverbs affirms that with "an abundance of counselors plans succeed" (Prov. 15:22, paraphrase).

## *"An Abundance"*

How many people should serve on the Search Committee? Opinions and church styles differ widely, but the optimum number seems to be between five and ten, with many choosing seven. A group of less than five can easily become dominated by one individual. Groups larger than ten can have so many diverse opinions that they will struggle to reach a consensus.

No matter what the final number on the Search Committee, one *hot issue* that will be affected by the size is unanimity. Will the Search Committee need to be unanimous about the person presented to the church, the ruling boards, or the Personnel Committee?

Churches can divide over this issue—especially if unanimity is decided upon as an ideal and one member of the committee consciously or unconsciously begins to wield power by being the dissenting vote.

To resolve this potential problem at the outset, one Search Committee recommends this procedure:

1. The ideal is unanimity, but the diversity of people on the Search Committee combined with the size of the committee may make this impossible.

2. Surround all of the Search Committee's activity with prayer. It is often God's way to clear out bad motives, divisive attitudes, and impatience.

3. Try to agree at the beginning on a general profile of the qualities and qualifications of the person being sought (see Part 4), and stick to this list.

4. Do not require unanimity on which candidates to interview or pursue. If someone fits the general profile, allow the interview/pursuit process to continue.

5. When the Search Committee is arriving at the final candidate, allow for disagreement through the use of a minority report (i.e., the feedback of those who might not endorse the majority's choice for a candidate). When the governing board (the next group involved in approving the candidate) hears both reports, it can decide whether or not to proceed with the candidate.

## *"Of Counselors"*

Who should be on this Search Committee? Parents? Teenagers? The senior minister? One person complained that the Search Committee on which he served had a group of people who "didn't understand kids and relational ministry." He added that choosing a youth pastor is "more than hearing the right doctrine from the person."

So what does a balanced and thorough Search Committee look like? Again, the opinions vary widely, but certain categories of people within the church should have some representation on this committee. Individuals and churches need to decide the best possible committee for their own situation, but Search Committees work best with a cross-section of the following people.

**Church leaders.** At least one member of the pastoral staff and/or the ruling lay board should sit on this committee. In our church, the youth ministry search process is chaired by the Minister of Christian Education, and the Overseeing Elder (our ruling board) assigned to the youth ministry also serves. In some churches, members of the Personnel Committee serve on a Search Committee so that questions about salary, housing, benefits, and budgets can be answered accurately.

Depending on church size, staff makeup, and church government, the senior minister may sit on this committee, serve in an ex officio capacity, or simply receive reports from the person chairing this committee. Related to the Search Committee's interaction with the senior pastor, consider another *hot issue* that the Search Committee will need to decide: how to keep the pastor informed and involved in the process (especially if the pastor has veto power over the selection of staff members).

The Search Committee can avoid an enormous amount of frustration if the relationship with the senior minister is clearly spelled out at the beginning of the process.

**Parents.** Concerned parents should definitely be represented on an effective Youth Pastor Search Committee. These folks usually have the greatest vested interest in the youth program, and their questions can be very perceptive in identifying a youth worker's capabilities in communication.

Try to avoid, however, parents who come with a hostile agenda:

- Those who are angry toward the previous youth pastor for some reason
- Those who are having significant problems reaching their own teenagers and are looking for a youth pastor who will bail them out
- Those who are long-term members of the church and romanticize the days of yesteryear when they were in the youth group

**Youths.** Some people think it's outrageous to consider involving a teenager or two on this committee, but the benefits far outweigh the difficulties. Involving a student on this committee tells the youth group that the church cares about how the young people think and feel. An effective student member can be responsible for surveying student needs and can often receive responses that no adult would receive.

Obviously, there are potential pitfalls. The youth member could be bullied by adults who nullify the student's opinions. The student who volunteers for this committee may not be the most equipped to serve.

One student member of a Youth Pastor Search Committee wrote about her experience being a "nightmare" because "for the first time I saw church politics in full swing. Young people serving on a church committee need to be fully prepared that they may see things which will upset and disillusion them."

In some situations, the best selection might be a student appointed by the most spiritually mature members of the youth group itself, one who can speak to the variety of needs represented in the youth group. In some churches, this person is the youth group president.

Another church, in an effort to involve youths in the search process, established a subcommittee of youths to serve the Search Committee. This sub-committee included representatives from the three major facets of the youth ministry who would be affected by a new youth pastor (middle school, high school, and college). The subcommittee solicited student opinion of what was needed in a youth leader, then compiled the results and presented them to the Search Committee. This action included youths in the process, informed the Search Committee, and communicated to the youths the adults' willingness to listen to their feedback and opinions.

**Volunteer youth leaders.** Adults who have served as leaders in the past or present youth ministry make a valuable contribution to the Search Committee. These people combine a working knowledge of the students with an understanding of the programming needs of the existing youth ministry. They can assist the Search Committee in identifying a big picture of the roles the youth pastor will need to fulfill.

**At-large members.** Many Search Committees leave room for one or two at-large members. These people may have no direct interest in or commitment to the youth program, but they can offer effective and *objective* insights in the search process. Some of the at-large possibilities to consider include the following:

- A youth expert. This person could be a former youth minister or a staff member of Campus Crusade for Christ's high school or college ministry. It might be a person serving with Young Life or Youth for Christ, or a staff member of Inter-Varsity Christian Fellowship. In general, this person understands the needs of contemporary youths and how a church youth ministry can respond.

- A person in the school system. Someone who teaches teenagers or administers in a school system can offer excellent insights on the youths in the local areas touched by the church.

- A youth or family counselor. In light of the fact that any youth minister will inherit scores of needy youths and their families, a counseling specialist can educate the committee about the needs a prospective youth pastor will face.

## *Toward Successful Planning*

Several other recommendations and guiding principles can foster the success of the Search Committee in its formative stages.

**Prepare the committee.** One associate pastor recommends that each member of the Search Committee take a personality test at the beginning of the search process. The DISC, LEAD, or Myers-

Briggs tests (with an interpretation offered by a trained person) can help the committee members understand how they are likely to interact.

**Don't mistake complaining for interest.** One church chose a Search Committee made up of all the people who complained the most about the youth ministry. That set a very negative tone at the outset, added needless arguments, and resulted in wasted time as some resigned and new members were assimilated.

**Make sure committee members understand their purpose.** One church leader advised me, "The point of the committee is to hire a youth pastor who can do the job, not have a spiritual experience together." He explained how the people on one church's Search Committee focused so much on the spiritual dynamics of their prayerful experience together that they took over two years in the process. They finally presented an ill-equipped candidate, the church hired the person out of frustration, and now the church is hurting.

**Go beyond the committee for support.** One creative church required each Search Committee member to raise three prayer supporters from the church family. The prayer supporters established a weekly prayer meeting where they committed themselves to pray for the Search Committee and for God's choice of the best candidate.

**Select members who will make the time.** The best Search Committee includes men and women who are praying, reading, and researching between meetings. In other words, the youth pastor search becomes a *priority* to them. The member who misses a lot of meetings or enters every meeting unprepared should be challenged or invited to resign.

**Commit to confidentiality.** A Search Committee functions best when everyone understands that confidentiality is a basic commitment. People and resumes can be discussed frankly and honestly without fear of information being "leaked" to the congregation.

**Commit to do the work.** An effective Search Committee understands that a rushed decision is often a poor decision. Thus, the Committee should be committed from the outset to do the hard work related to the search. One corollary here: in general, the larger the ministry, the longer the search. Larger ministries often take longer to determine future direction, which, combined with a greater demand for experienced leaders, often extends the search process.

**Commit to communicate.** The Search Committee must be committed to keeping the church leaders, the youths, the parents, and the church at large informed of its progress. Periodic reports in major services or newsletters to the congregation may be effective ways to do this. Communication in the process averts an adversarial reaction from the church leaders and the congregation when the final candidate is presented.

## Part 3

# The Questions

We all know the stories of people who marched forward with a plan without really counting the cost before building. They were so excited about some idea or ideal that they went ahead naively, only to encounter trouble later. Unfulfilled dreams, incomplete projects, and mismatched solutions are the result.

The same can happen in the selection of a youth pastor. When we were looking for a youth pastor several years ago, a Search Committee member visited the youth pastor in charge of a large ministry in the southern United States. His ministry included over five hundred students, met in their own reconditioned warehouse, and included paid staff people in charge of the youth ministry music and media. The person returned and excitedly presented the minister he had met as our "ideal" youth ministry candidate. He was enamored with what he saw and assumed that the youth leader could reproduce his ministry in our community.

Unfortunately, the Search Committee member forgot to ask some basic background questions about his ideal candidate's situation versus ours. He managed a larger youth ministry budget than anything we could ever offer, and he operated his youth ministry in a culture that was not quite as secularized as ours. Various other factors also differed dramatically.

Our Search Committee member needed to discern how to address some of the introductory issues that will affect the search. He needed to understand issues that the committee should wrestle with *before* actually identifying specific candidates.

## Chapter 3

# What Is Our Church's Youth Ministry History?

Church history affects the Search Committee because it helps determine expectations. Identifying the history will help the Search Committee avoid some of the faulty expectations coinciding with that history. Then the committee can proceed to produce expectations that are realistic, balanced, and relevant to the times.

## *In Search of the Messiah*

In a church with no youth ministry history or a church that has never employed a person as a youth pastor, the temptation is often to look for a Messiah or a superhuman who will fulfill all of the church's dreams concerning youth ministry.

A pastor wrote to me with the exciting news that his church had decided to pursue the hiring of their first-ever youth minister. He told me that several committees had gathered to brainstorm about the position, and they had drafted a job description. The pastor asked me to look over the job description and offer feedback. I agreed.

His letter came with an attached job description: it was three pages, single-spaced, and put the youth minister into direct ministry with young people ages ten to early twenties. At first, I wanted to ask sarcastically, "And *how many* people are you hiring to fill this position?" But I resisted the temptation.

Instead, I pointed out that their expectations were probably too high. Either they needed to focus the job to one or two of their specific youth groupings, or they needed to expand the job to associate pastor and give that associate oversight responsibilities for five or six ministries that would be led by lay volunteers or perhaps per-time interns. The person they were looking for simply did not exist.

## *The Pendulum Effect*

I served our church as youth pastor for ten years. Throughout those years, my work was affirmed for its organization, its utilization of volunteers, its discipling emphasis, and its world missions outreach. But all was not perfect. The consistent (and

30

legitimate) critiques were that I did not have enough music and did not have enough direct youth outreach to the "fringe" (or alienated) students in the community and the church.

When I resigned, the Search Committee immediately drafted its list of hopes for my successor. What topped the list? More music, more ministry to fringe kids, more outreach in the community.

Our church followed the typical pattern of Search Committees (for all positions, not just youth pastors): look for someone who will make up for the shortcomings of the predecessor. Churches that have recently lost a youth worker recruit to make up for earlier weaknesses.

Our church hired a youth pastor who was musical, outreach-oriented, and great at reaching the fringe students. The church gained the skills that made up for my weaknesses but also lost some things: intensive discipleship ministry waned, the Sunday school suffered, and summer mission trips lost their focus.

The pendulum swings from extreme to extreme. Search Committees need to understand the tendency to act reactively. Imagine these observations being made by Search Committee members:

- "Our past youth pastor was very relational, but he was so disorganized. We need an administrator."

- "Doug really poured his heart out for the kids, but he had very little interaction with or ministry to families. We need someone who will work with parents, not just kids."

- "Maureen did a good job, but I think we need a man in that position." This same statement could be made by someone reacting to issues of *age* (someone "older and more mature" versus "younger and more energetic" than the predecessor), *marital status* (someone "single with more time to give" versus "married and setting an example" in contrast to the previous youth pastor), or even *family status* (a youth pastor who is childless versus another who has three children under age six).

## *In the Shadow of the Legend*

Bob took me to the Fellowship Hall of his church to explain why his new position as youth pastor was going poorly. He asked, "Do you see that picture on the center wall?" It was a group picture taken about 1928 of a hundred Scandinavian-looking young people in front of the church building.

"That picture," Bob explained, "represents the greatest youth ministry this church has ever known, and everyone still wonders why neither I nor my predecessors have been able to re-create it.

"When that group was in this church, everyone lived within a few blocks, came from the same stock of immigrants, and was generally a nice person trying to be better. One of the hottest issues of the day was whether or not to allow gum chewing in the church. The youths we reach now are multiracial, urban, and often associated with gangs. I'm fighting guns, not gum."

Bob's church is locked in on a legend, and effective youth ministry will never occur until the church changes its perspective—appreciating the past but adjusting to the reality of the times. Churches that had an effective youth ministry or youth pastor many years ago often face the temptation of looking for a youth leader who will fulfill the expectations of a romanticized past.

## *The Search Committee's Responses*

In the early stages of the search for a new youth pastor, the Search Committee can ensure forward progress by making two responses to the research on the church's youth ministry history.

**Response 1.** Identifying the strengths and weaknesses of the church's past efforts with young people helps the Search Committee understand where it is coming from, what some of the church's legacies are regarding youth ministry, and which positive strengths of youth ministry past can be built on in preparing for the future.

**Response 2.** Simultaneous with an understanding of the past must be a response directed toward the future. The Search Committee should ask, What strengths will our youth ministry need to exhibit if we are to reach the youths of today and tomorrow? This question is developed later in chapter 9, "Where Are We Now and Where Do We Want the Youth Ministry to Go?"

These responses help the Search Committee celebrate the past without getting locked into repeating it.

## Chapter 4

# What Is Our Church Culture?

The church's youth ministry history relates closely to the *very* important issue of church culture. Whether we admit it or not, our churches have certain cultures that are a by-product of the culture around us, the theology of the church, the history of the church, and the socioeconomic dynamics within the congregation.

Living in New England all of my life and serving for the past twenty years in an interdenominational church of over two thousand people from ninety communities and a wide range of socioeconomic backgrounds, *I know* how important church culture is in affecting the direction of the youth ministry and the style of youth minister needed.

Our church culture demands that a youth worker be able to relate to a large number of high schools (at last count, we drew students from over forty schools). Thus, a youth leader focused on reaching *the* school of the community will not do well in our church's culture.

Most of our students come from middle- or upper-middle-class families with parents who have bachelor's or master's degrees. They expect that their high schoolers will go on to college. Thus, a youth worker at our church must pay attention to the perceived academic needs of students in order to fit the church culture.

A variety of other factors make up church culture. The Search Committee should take into account these issues in evaluating the church culture.

## *Geography and the Outside Culture*

*The Nine Nations of North America* explains how the industrial and cultural histories of the regions of North America have formed some of the subcultural distinctives affecting those areas and the church.[1] Some regions are wide open to new ideas; others are conservative and slow to change. Some areas are gregarious and outgoing; others are reserved, even cold, toward outsiders. Although the movement of our mobile society has blurred some of these subcultural lines, the fact remains: the country is *not* some sort of homogenous cultural pie, and our churches aren't, either.

Just ask Phil and Marie. They came from Arkansas to study in New England in preparation for missionary service in South America. In their own words, "the cultural jump from Arkansas to New England was far more difficult for us than the adjustments from the United States to Latin America."

Others would echo their discovery about cultural differences within the North American regions. Rich moved from the Pacific Northwest to the Deep South. Fran took her family from New York to southern California. Mike and Anne Marie came to Grace Chapel in suburban Boston from a small town in Oklahoma. All have discovered that the culture of the region and the culture of the church combine to add to the challenges of adjustment.

I grew up seven miles from Grace Chapel. When I graduated from seminary, our pastor urged me to stay as the youth pastor: "If we bring someone here from some other part of the country, it will take the person at least two years to adjust to the culture."

I knew he was correct. I had met with fellow seminarians from other parts of the country to help them through their culture shock. Several had come from the Midwest where they had led Young Life or Youth for Christ ministries. They were accustomed to going on high school campuses, announcing a "Club" meeting on Saturday night, and getting two hundred students to attend. When they came to northeastern Massachusetts, they were refused access to the high school as they tried to reach out to the young people who viewed their enthusiasm with suspicion and who had never heard of Young Life or Youth for Christ.

Church culture overlaps with the issue of youth culture in the area. A lay leader in southeastern Connecticut wrote to tell me of a church in his area that recently hired a youth pastor from Minnesota: "He is a nice guy, but he and his wife are midwesterners who have never lived in the East. They are out of place with the affluent, eastern, preppy culture in this area. Can he do the job?"

The most important thing is that we not be naive about cultural differences when we interview candidates. People can and do make effective cultural transitions all of the time. Tim brought his southern accent and hospitality with him from North Carolina and served our church's youth ministry effectively for five years. Vic moved from Atlantic Canada to Indiana. Beth left her Minnesota home and settled effectively in Texas.

Search Committees need to be familiar with the culture in their region and then ask, Can this candidate make the transition?

**Urban versus suburban/rural.** The differences here are obvious. Urban youth workers often are involved in more people-intensive ministries; that is, they have small groups, but the young people are dealing with tougher challenges in their neighborhoods or schools. In his work with urban Young Life, Chris's ministry has never grown very large, but he is deeply involved with parole programs and counseling students who are trying to leave gangs. He is tutoring students in an effort to keep them from dropping out of high school.

Suburban and rural youth workers often concentrate on more program-intensive youth ministries. They may work with more students, but their ministries will combine personal discipleship with administering a significant youth ministry program designed to be a Christian alternative for the church's students.

The Search Committee should identify the predominant type of youth ministry that the church culture needs before evaluating potential youth ministry candidates.

**Socioeconomics.** The social setting and economic status of the church will also affect the church culture. A friend in youth ministry works in Orange County, California—one of the wealthiest areas of the United States. Most of the older students (juniors and seniors in high school) in his church own cars, have traveled internationally with their families, and have pools at their homes. He works in a church culture where students miss youth group meetings because they have lessons at the riding academy.

Another youth ministry friend works in an urban church with poorer students. He works to encourage the older students in his group to stay in school or work toward high school equivalency diplomas. They have never traveled, and the city pool might be their only recreational option in the summer. If students miss a meeting, he fears that they are in trouble with a gang.

These examples illustrate extremes, but they show how socioeconomics affects the church culture, the youth group, and the type of youth pastor appropriate for the church. One youth pastor trains college-bound high schoolers how to use their daily planning calendars. Another ministers with latchkey youths from blue-collar families who desperately hope that she will fill their weekends with great programs.

The type of youth ministry being done reflects the socioeconomic culture of the church.

## *Theology/Church Tradition*

A Youth Pastor Search Committee may look outside its denomination or tradition for the best possible candidates, but that does not mean theology and tradition are insignificant.

A Presbyterian church may desire a man with proven experience as the youth pastor, but if he is a Baptist who tries to immerse the youth group on his first retreat, the church is in for a crisis. Those from more Pentecostal/charismatic traditions may not do well with a youth minister from a high church tradition.

The movement in churches across North America is toward a more interdenominational spirit; experts like George Barna predict that "denominational brand loyalty" is on the decline. As a result, the controversial doctrinal distinctives may not be as significant as they once were, but every Search Committee must be sure to understand where the church leaders will compromise and where their convictions will not be shaken.

Is it the person's escatology? We once rejected a ministerial candidate who wanted to force his brand of teaching on the end times on our church, which does not insist on or advocate any one of the many systems.

Is it the issue of raising hands in worship? The youths of one church criticized the worship as being dead. When the new youth pastor (who advocated a more charismatic style of worship) tried to infuse some life into the church, he was seen as being divisive and taking sides with the high schoolers.

Is it speaking in tongues—either privately or in corporate worship? One volunteer youth leader created a crisis in a conservative, fundamentalist church when he took the youth group on a field trip where they all (including the pastor's son!) received the baptism of the Holy Spirit and the gift of tongues.

The Search Committee's failure to identify these theological issues up front can lead to the hiring of a youth pastor who will either contradict church doctrine or form the youth group into a divisive minichurch within the church.

To avoid such conflicts, the Search Committee must not shy away from controversial questions during the interviewing of candidates, for example, "Would you be willing to abide by our traditions or convictions in this matter?"

(Note: The Search Committee can save time here by making sure that the church's statement of faith is sent to each applicant in the initial application process. That will allow theological issues to surface early, which might cause someone to withdraw as a candidate.)

## NOTE

1. Joel Garreau, *The Nine Nations of North America* (New York: Avon Books, 1982).

## Chapter 5

# Do We Understand the Philosophy of Church Youth Ministry?

———◆———

The Search Committee will do best with an understanding of the various philosophical approaches to youth ministry, especially the contrast between church youth ministry and parachurch youth ministry.

If Search Committee members understand the philosophical position for themselves and the church, the choice of a youth pastor who blends with that philosophy will be much easier.[1]

## Roy's Story

After seven years on the staff of Youth for Christ, my friend Roy entered seminary. He wanted a better theological foundation for ministry and a youth ministry position in a local church.

While attending seminary, Roy took several youth ministry courses and attended two conferences on youth ministry in an effort to stay fresh. When he graduated, he became an associate minister at a church within his denomination. He was responsible for the youth groups, with additional part-time preaching, counseling, and visitation duties.

When Roy began working with the youth groups, he felt prepared. His philosophical and theological "guns" were loaded. He had lots of ideas for programs. He was ready to go. That was September.

By late November, Roy was *very* discouraged. A few months of flat programming, disinterested kids, and hassles from parents had tired him out. On November 22, he wrote in his diary: "Working with church youth is more difficult than I ever expected."

Youth ministry in the local church differs from the ministries of the parachurch organizations. It differs from the idealistic models often presented in manuals and seminars.

## How Is Church Youth Ministry Different?

The first step toward solving the problems inherent in local church youth ministry is identifying the tensions that youth ministers and leaders will face. In what way is *church* ministry to young people unique?

**The responsibilities are different.** When Roy accepted the position of associate minister, he took on a host of responsibilities unrelated to youth ministry. Preparation for a monthly sermon, six to eight hours per week of counseling, and two or three trips to the hospital each week were reminders that young people were not his only focus. The other duties competed for his time and attention.

While all leaders work within systems of relationships, authority, and communication, tensions arise for the youth minister because the systems are often broader and larger. My friend John, a Young Life staff member, has one superior to whom he reports. He has one boss. The church youth worker, on the other hand, has one superior on the organizational chart but also has parents, elders (or deacons), and sometimes even the young people themselves who function as superiors.

The complexity of relationships and the anxiety of multiple responsibilities are in direct conflict with much that is taught or written about youth ministry. Many youth ministry ideals assume that the leader has forty or more hours per week to dedicate to youth work; that is seldom the case in church ministry.

**The kids are different.** Remember Roy? One factor that discouraged him most in his ministry was disinterested kids. Young people, while representing a great resource of the church, are also a great challenge to the church.

First, the kids may be "Christianized." Many of the kids in church youth groups come from Christian families, they have always attended Sunday school, and some may even attend a Christian school. These students know the Bible stories, can repeat doctrines verbatim, and can give pat answers to even the most thought-provoking questions. As a result, youth workers face the challenges of working with young people who say, "I dare you to teach me anything new."

Second, some teenagers from Christian families may attend the youth groups against their will. They come into a youth group meeting, sit in the back row, and fold their arms. They may write notes, talk to their friends, or sleep. When asked if they want to be in the youth group, they reply, "No, but our parents told us that if we want to be able to go out other nights, we have to go to youth group." Any way you look at it, these students enter the group through circumstances that will not make life easy for their youth leaders. Progress will be difficult.

Third, the interrelationship between the church and the youth group means that the youth leader will be the target of many parental hopes or demands: "We are really looking forward to the changes you can make in our children." One youth minister was asked why he was spending time with a rebellious youth who had abandoned his parents' faith two years earlier. He said the church elders had told him that the youth's parents had served in the church so faithfully that the church was obligated to try to reach the boy. Such pressures on the youth minister made his job very demanding.

Problems with teenagers in the youth group may be compounded if the youth minister is just another in a succession of youth ministers. The high turnover of youth workers in the local church often means that the responsiveness in many young people has been destroyed through broken relationships and unfulfilled promises.

**The task is different.** Jack, a veteran youth worker with a local parachurch ministry, spends up to four days per week meeting with unchurched students, sharing the gospel message. Church youth workers usually can't do this without being accused of abandoning the young people of the church. The primary task of the parachurch organization is evangelism; the task of the church youth worker is nurturing.

For the church youth worker, the challenge is to work with those who know the gospel intellectually but who need to personalize the faith of their parents. Taking teenagers through this painstaking and gradual process demands commitment and patience. This commitment to nurturing is made even more complex because the church youth leader must be versatile in reaching teenagers who are on a variety of spiritual levels. Many youth groups will include the *disillusioned* (who want nothing to do with Christianity), the *searchers* (who want to know God but don't know how), the *fence sitters* (who, like chameleons, modify their behavior to fit their environment), the *neutrals* (whose apathy about everything makes it difficult to know what they believe), and the *disciples* (whose zeal to follow Jesus often alienates them from their peers).

The leader's versatility is further tested as students fluctuate across the spiritual spectrum on a weekly or monthly basis. The task of the church youth minister then becomes the patient tracking of these young people until they come to a firm commitment to Jesus Christ and to the pursuit of a Christian life-style.

## *Positive Steps for a Philosophy of Church Youth Ministry*

Recognizing the unique aspects of church youth work is only the first step toward effective discipleship, growth, and outreach. The Search Committee can respond to these unique aspects of church youth ministry by defining the target, role, and goal of the youth pastor in accordance with church realities.

**Define the youth pastor's target: the church's young people.** Tim has an incredible youth ministry. He leads a discipleship Bible study with the church youths and an evangelistic group at the local high school; he coordinates separate programs for the churched and the unchurched because he recognizes the different needs of the two groups. Tim is an exceptional man; he is also very tired.

Most youth pastors have to decide whether to work with the church's young people or with the unchurched. Youth leaders do not have the abilities, gifts, or time to do both. Yet many in church youth ministry are sometimes afraid of stating, "I am called by God to work with *church* youths." Perhaps youth pastors fear the implications, or they worry that someone will accuse them of losing their burden for the unsaved. Nevertheless, effective youth ministry in the church requires that the church's young people become the priority and the focus. This concentration, however, carries with it certain weighty implications.

This mind-set implies a willingness to accept and work within the church system mentioned earlier. Any outgoing youth pastor would love to visit the high school campuses every day, but a church job requires her to maintain the youth budget, plan the hayride, book the speaker for the retreat, go to the staff meeting, attend the evening service, meet with the elders, or write a staff report. The system in which God has placed the youth minister means taking all of the church responsibilities into account as he sets personal and ministry goals.

Making the church's young people a priority also implies a commitment to work with parents and families. Like Tim Jack, high school pastor at Grace Community Church in Sun Valley, California, we must see our ministries in the context of families. As he stated in an interview, "We are seeking to help families in their ministry to youth, not to replace it with ours."[2]

This commitment can be frightening at times. For example, a father was very angry with me because his sixteen-year-old son was not witnessing for Christ at his high school. I knew that I could be silent and take the blows, or I could overcome my fears and speak the truth. I spoke up: "Sir, do you witness to your friends at work?" He mumbled something about everyone already knowing he was a Christian. I reminded him that unless he was willing to set an example, it would be very difficult for me to get his son to do evangelism. Effective ministry to the students requires courageous ministry with the parents.

Commitment to the church's young people requires patience with them as they grow. Christian teenagers are curious, and the sheltered environment they are raised in often increases this curiosity about what "the world" is really like. As a result, they might experiment and test the waters of the secular world while they profess to follow Christ. This spiritual inconsistency should be challenged, but the ability to be merciful and understanding of students' curiosity is also important.

Finally, a stated commitment to the church's young people implies the support of the other leaders in the church. Bernie, a church youth minister, has an effective ministry to the church's teens, but he lives under the constant pressure of comparison with the local area's Campus Life outreach. Were it not for the complete support and encouragement of the church's other pastors and the lay leaders, Bernie probably would move on to another church.

Effective ministry to the church's teenagers requires that others in the church recognize that working with the youth group is a demanding job and requires the youth leader's primary attention. If the church expects the youth worker to give 100 percent to church growth and 100 percent to outreach, the youth worker will face an impossible and unreachable goal.

**Define the youth minister's role: pastor to youths.** A youth pastor from a very large youth ministry once challenged me, "Are we the *pastor* to our youths?" If we are, he insisted, we should equip *them* to do their own God-given ministries.

This helpful piece of biblical advice (according to Eph. 4:11–13) can transform the perspective of the youth pastor and the youth ministry. Instead of trying to be everything to the youth ministry, the youth leader is responsible to be the pastor to youths, the equipper. The responsibility is to teach students, to exemplify a Christian life-style, and to pray for them so that they—as members of the body of Christ, which the Christian students are— can do their ministry. Instead of being docile observers who are entertained and cajoled, students

51

become the active participants who "own" the ministry.

When I served as a youth pastor, I shared my vision with our high school students every September. I shared my dreams for evangelism at their high school campuses, and then I explained my role as equipper: "It isn't my job to reach these students. It *is* my job to make sure that *you* are equipped to do this outreach. Reaching these students is your responsibility. If you aren't equipped, I am failing. But if you are equipped and you don't act, the failure is yours."

This changed definition of my role brought greater joy and fulfillment as I had the opportunity to see students rise to the challenge. Seeing Andy teach Sunday school or seeing Brett start his own evangelistic Bible study gave me much greater joy than doing it myself. The joy that John expressed in seeing his "children walk in truth" (3 John 4) is available to the youth minister who equips young people to do their own ministries.

**Define the youth pastor's goal: to challenge youths for growth.** Persons in church youth work are always in danger of compromising the goals of teaching and admonishing (Col. 1:28) by trying to gauge success by other measures. However, stimulating teens to grow toward completeness in Christ means resisting this temptation.

Some youth workers (motivated at times by pressure from church leaders) fall prey to the compromise of entertainment. They convince themselves that a bigger and better program (with large crowds, of course) is synonymous with success with young people. A problem emerges, however, when it becomes apparent that the quality of the entertainment—rather than a commitment to Christ—has become the criterion for attendance and participation.

Perry had an active program that reached 250 or more teenagers, but he cut his program way back. Why? "I realized that pulling off the program was becoming the goal," he said, "and I saw my fellow leaders expending all of their energies there rather than in ministry to the kids."

Other youth leaders fall prey to compromise because they become preoccupied with popularity. I am almost forty years old, twenty years out of high school, and happily married—yet it really bothers me when a teenager in my youth group doesn't like me. I try to argue with myself: Why does this bother me? I don't need the approval of a fifteen-year-old! But it still bothers me. I like to be liked. Most people-oriented youth leaders do.

The compromise occurs when the youth worker lets this desire to be liked by the kids (and their parents) overcome the biblical priorities of growth, challenge, and accountability. An effective youth leader knows that he cannot be everyone's buddy. Productive ministry to young people in the church context requires that the youth minister define her priorities clearly. Experiencing Christian growth is more important than being entertained. Being the leader is more important than being liked. When these priorities are defined, youth pastors are free to challenge students and parents to grow toward maturity in Christ.

Students need to know that following Christ isn't fun and games or a search for self-fulfillment. Following Christ demands commitment; following Christ is costly. Charles Atlas coined the phrase, "No pain; no gain." Young people believe it. They are willing to practice through the grueling summer heat to play football. They will spend all of their money and much of their time to pursue their desire to play guitars or synthesizers. They believe that a worthwhile goal is worth the cost.

If the church's young people are not met with the challenge to follow Christ, they will seek challenges elsewhere. We in the church must not be afraid to present the commitment and cost of following Christ. At times, the youth group may decrease in size, but the depth of growth in the students will surpass our expectations.

In 1978, we started teen mission teams at our church. We didn't know how our young people would accept the concept of paying for the opportunity to work, so we proceeded slowly. They had to write a brief testimony and raise half the trip's cost. Over the years these teams have grown, largely because we have added more and more challenge each year. Now students have to raise all their support; they have to write an application and four other reports; they have to participate in a training weekend; they have to memorize Scripture, recruit prayer supporters, and speak in services. Some summers, over 80 percent of our high school students have applied for teams. The basic rule has proven itself: the more we challenge them, the more they respond and grow as a result.

## *Is This the Church's Philosophy?*

Youth ministry in the local church *is* different. We no doubt have much to learn from the expertise of the parachurch youth professionals and the nationwide seminars.

A Search Committee seeking the best leader for local church youth ministry, however, must go a few steps further. The unique aspects of the church, the young people, and the ministry must be identified, implemented, and integrated into the specific setting to find the person divinely called to youth ministry in the challenging but uniquely satisfying environment of the local church.

### NOTES

1. This chapter is a revision of a previously published article I wrote: "Church Youth Ministry: A Breed Apart," *Youthworker*, Spring 1984, pp. 76–80.

2. From an interview with Tim Jack in *Youthletter*, April 1983, p. 31.

## Chapter 6

# Are We Looking for a Youth Pastor or an Associate with Youth Responsibilities?

**A** survey by GROUP magazine revealed that 87 percent of persons in charge of youth ministry programs were paid church workers. Of those, however, only 19 percent were full-time youth workers (i.e., youth ministry was their *only* focus). Others were pastors with responsibility for youth work (24 percent), church staff members with responsibility for youth work (23 percent), and part-time paid church staff members (12 percent).[1]

The expectations we hold for a full-time youth pastor differ from those we can hold for someone who is running the youth ministry in fifteen hours per week and doing other Christian education or related ministry the rest of the time.

A full-time youth pastor is usually desirable (simply because of the intensity involved in student ministry), but many churches cannot afford one. Thus, each church must decide the full-time versus part-time question. There are corresponding benefits in either category.

A full-time youth pastor

- can be the church's expert focused on adolescents.
- can give the young people a greater sense of belonging and being a church priority.
- can work with parents and thus attract families to the church.
- can work in outreach to young people who are most likely to respond to the gospel (some estimate that 80 percent of those who become Christians do so before the age of eighteen).
- can integrate youths into the church leadership.

On the other hand, a pastor with other responsibilities

- can involve more people in leadership because she is more likely to recruit lay volunteers to help with the students.

- can involve students in other ministry in the church rather than create a youth group culture, which functions apart from the church.
- can save the church money because he is handling multiple responsibilities.

## *So How Do We Decide?*

While no exact formulas exist to determine the need for a youth pastor who is full-time in youth ministry versus someone who also handles other church responsibilities, considering five issues should help the Search Committee decide its basic direction.

**1. Church history.** If the church has traditionally had a full-time youth pastor, it will be very difficult for the next youth pastor to function effectively with divided responsibilities. On the other hand, if there has never been a full-time youth pastor, it may be difficult to convince the church that one is needed. In this case, someone who is hired with other responsibilities in the job description might be more acceptable to the church.

**2. The youth group size.** A youth group of twenty-five students or fewer can usually be led by a part-timer fairly effectively, but when the group is much larger, the demands of students and their families mean that the part-timer may be able to do little more than maintain the ministry.

**3. The church's priorities/budget.** Obviously, the budget is often the determining factor in whether or not a full-time youth pastor can be hired. Church leaders will often state, "Our budget will simply not allow it," and that may be true, but the Search Committee must highlight the fact that the budget is a reflection of the church's *priorities*. If youth ministry is a church priority, the budget should reflect it, both by salaries and by a supporting budget for the ministry.

**4. The nature and priority of other responsibilities.** If the youth pastor is being hired to do two unrelated tasks, the likelihood of success is less than if the tasks are interrelated. For example, a person responsible for youth and Christian education has interrelated tasks; in most churches, the youth department is part of Christian education. On the other hand, I served for three years as the minister of youth and missions, a job that grew to be increasingly divergent and resulted in both the youth and the missions departments suffering from neglect.

In any situation where the youth leader has multiple pastoral responsibilities, youth workers generally agree that *young people will suffer if the youth ministry is not considered one of the pastor's top two responsibilities.* In other words, youth groups that fall into the "and if you get to it" category in a pastor's job description will suffer.

**5. The pool of volunteers.** Who else is available to help in the youth department? One church successfully leads a youth program through a pastor who maintains partial youth ministry responsibility. He works through volunteers who are intensely committed to the group (most average over ten hours per week). Most of these volunteers, however, are youth ministry majors at a local Christian college. His pool of volunteers is extraordinary; most churches are not so fortunate.

## *The Issue of Titles*

Related to this question of part-time or full-time ministry leadership, the Search Committee should be clear about whether the church seeks a youth *minister* or a youth *director*. Although titles may not seem important to the Search Committee, the choice of titles can communicate a subtle message to the potential candidate.

The title of *minister* or *pastor* communicates that the person is being sought out as a full member of the pastoral staff. It says, "We see you as a spiritual leader in the church."

Youth *director*, on the other hand, seems to indicate that the youth leader is seen not as a pastor or shepherd but as a coordinator. Ridge Burns refers to this distinction in *Create in Me a Youth Ministry*: "Somehow the term *director* implied programming to me and the word *pastor* implied ministry, on which I place a higher value. It still bothers me—and other youth ministry professionals—to feel degraded because we've given our lives to students."[2]

## NOTES

1. Eugene C. Roehlkepartain, ed., *The Youth Ministry Resource Book* (Loveland, Colo.: GROUP Books, 1988), p. 184.

2. Ridge Burns with Pam Campbell, *Create in Me a Youth Ministry* (Wheaton: Victor Books, 1986), p. 45.

## Chapter 7

# How Do We Define
# *Youths?*

Although we will discuss the specific sphere of the youth pastor's responsibilities later, we need to start with at least a general focus. To whom are we referring as we talk about youths? Teenagers? Collegians? Singles? Elementary school children?

The group called adolescents is usually considered the primary focus of the youth pastor. These young people are in the phase somewhere between childhood and adulthood. Their bodies might be adult, but their minds and emotions are not fully mature yet. In general, adolescents are the distinct subculture aspiring to independence from parents but maintaining financial and emotional dependence on them.

In the past, *adolescents* and *teenagers* were almost synonymous. In the nineties and beyond, experts predict that the adolescent culture will continue to affect children much younger than teenagers and young adults well into their twenties. So what group is the youth pastor coming to reach: all adolescents or only teenagers?

The same *GROUP* magazine survey cited earlier identified the various areas of responsibility handled by people in youth ministry:

- 89 percent—high school ministry
- 88 percent—junior high (or middle school) ministry
- 38 percent—college ministry
- 41 percent—children's ministry
- 30 percent—young adult ministry[1]

The bottom line? Many youth workers were handling a broader range of responsibilities than teenagers, and most were dealing with at least two of the subgroups (junior high and senior high) most commonly included in teenage-focused youth ministry.

So what is the focus of the committee's search?

## *A Broad Focus Versus a Tight Focus*

Before deciding the final answer to this, the Search Committee should review some of the questions raised in chapter 6 concerning multiple responsibilities for the youth pastor. Even if the desired target of the youth pastor is specifically youths, the Search Committee should weigh some of the pros and cons associated with how that youth ministry will be focused.

**A broad focus.** For example, a youth pastor is responsible for junior high, senior high, and college ministry.

**Pros:**

- Greater continuity is afforded for youths and parents as young people grow up.
- The youth pastor has a broad knowledge of student ministry.
- This option is realistic for most churches with respect to budgets and programs.
- More adults are required to get involved as supportive helpers.

**Cons:**

- The youth pastor is spread too thin.
- The youth pastor inevitably must choose one realm of involvement (high school ministry, for example), which can leave the other groups feeling second-class.
- The youth pastor may be forced to bounce from group to group, thus diffusing impact and focus.
- The youth pastor looks to volunteers primarily as those who maintain a program rather than those who are developed as the pastors to the young people.
- The youth pastor is so involved maintaining the groups that little attention can be dedicated to outreach.

**A tight focus.** For example, a youth pastor is totally dedicated to junior high ministry.

## Pros:

- The youth pastor's efforts are concentrated on reaching and discipling one specific group.
- The youth pastor becomes an expert on that specific aspect of youth culture.
- The youth pastor can develop the volunteer team into a strong group dedicated to pastoring the targeted group.

## Cons:

- The youth group can lack continuity if there are three or more leaders in the youth ministry.
- The youth subgroup can become too focused, turning it into its own church and making it difficult for young people to make the transition to the next group.
- The church's financial investment in youth ministry might be considered too high.

The Search Committee must decide before painting the picture of the Youth Pastor Profile because either choice (a broad focus or a tight one) will affect the type of youth minister to seek.

### NOTE

1. Eugene C. Roehlkepartain, ed., *The Youth Ministry Resource Book* (Loveland, Colo.: GROUP Books, 1988), p. 184.

## Chapter 8

# What Can a Youth Pastor Really Offer?

Jim Petipas has served in youth ministry for several years, and he now pastors our church's junior high ministry. In a humorous approach to addressing the expectations associated with youth ministry, Jim contrasts the "totaled" youth worker with the "total" youth worker.

**The "totaled" youth worker** is characterized by

- brain fried from trying to come up with new youth ministry ideas.
- shoulders stooped from carrying the load alone.
- belt tight due to lack of available funds.
- hands empty and ready to grasp at any youth program that will work.

- knees calloused from prayers of desperation for uncommitted teens.
- clothes messy because of lack of attention to personal needs.
- feet sore from running all over town looking for youth program material.
- hair pulled out from trying to decide what to do at the next youth meeting.
- eyes bloodshot from lying awake at night worrying.
- heart aching to reach out to unchurched teens.
- watch with no time available for much youth ministry preparation.
- fingernails bitten down from worrying about youth ministry.

In general, most Search Committees would agree that this burned-out individual is not the person to meet a church's needs. Instead, most are looking for the "total" youth worker.

**The "total" youth worker** is characterized by

- brain filled with the newest total program ideas.
- shoulders straight and strong due to total confidence.
- belt tightened, but it doesn't matter because of commitment to the total cost of youth ministry.
- hands firmly wrapped around the total youth ministry package.
- knees calloused from prayers of praise for total success.
- clothes conveying an overall neat appearance due to attention to personal enrichment.

- feet rested; no more running around; this person's got it all together.
- eyes focused on the goal—building the kingdom.
- face bright due to a successful ministry.
- heart filled with joy because new students are coming.
- watch that keeps this person on time because schedule is managed with total efficiency.
- fingers that have walked through all of the resources and found the best materials available.

Jim's tongue-in-cheek description of two extremes in youth workers highlights the tension associated with the search for the ideal youth minister versus the real individuals who come to the attention of the Search Committee. These people, gifted as they might be, come with their limitations and flaws. From this group, the Search Committee will need to choose the next youth pastor.

## *Realistic Expectations*

As a result of this tension, the Search Committee needs an honest appraisal of what a potential youth pastor can bring to the church. What types of programs, discipleship, counseling, and ministry to parents can one person bring to the formative or existing youth ministry? Inflated expectations of youth pastors need to be tempered. Those doing the searching need to be realistic.

Tom McLaughlin, a former Grace Chapel youth ministry intern and veteran of youth ministry leadership in three churches, points to expectations as a key issue for Search Committees: "The most centrally important consideration for whatever type of Search Committee/board to address seems to revolve around *expectations*—the expectations the church has for the youth pastor as well as the expectations the youth pastor has for the church. Once these can be identified with a reasonable degree of agreement, you've got a good 'fit.'"

Expectations vary according to the church size and the church leaders' desires for the youth ministry. The smaller church that hires a pastoral associate who will dedicate 25 percent of the time to minister to junior highers, senior highers, and collegians will have very different expectations from the church that hires a full-time pastor for middle school youths. The former should expect some programs, a team of lay volunteers coached by the pastoral associate, and youth ministry that might be healthy but probably will not grow significantly. The latter should expect direct ministry, focused efforts with a specific age group, and other specialized ministry (mission teams, parent support groups, etc.).

Wayne Rice of Youth Specialties Ministries advises Search Committees, "Don't expect too much, especially if you are hiring a youth minister who will be expected to lead the entire youth ministry alone (which is still the most common model, even though it's probably not correct). Decide in advance what one thing you would like for him or her to do. He may not know how to organize a youth mission trip. She may not be the best speaker in the world. But what are your top priorities for the youth ministry? Is she an excellent counselor? Can he lead worship? Is this what you want? Very few youth workers can do everything. Decide what you want and don't expect success in other areas."

## *The Bottom Line*

The temptation will be to search for a superhuman to fill the multiple expectations of the Search Committee, the church leaders, the youths, and the parents. At the outset, members of the Search Committee should say aloud together, "This person does not exist!"

Once the Search Committee accepts that it is looking for a faithful youth worker who will be the best possible fit with the church, the committee is freed from the hunt for a Messiah figure who will be everything everyone wants and more. From this point of reality, the Search Committee can start drawing up the profile of the desired youth pastor.

## Part 4

# The Profile of
# the Youth Pastor

To manage the search process and determine the best fit of youth pastor and church, the Search Committee should design a profile paper outlining the goals, aspirations, and expectations of persons who will be considered as youth pastor.

The questions in Part 3 have already started this process, and the questionnaires and resources in the Appendixes can add structure to the process.

In general, the Search Committee wants to produce a profile paper that looks like this:

## SAMPLE YOUTH PASTOR PROFILE

This sample was adapted from a profile created by the Youth Pastor Search Committee of the Mitchell Road Presbyterian Church in Greenville, South Carolina.

*Experience:* Minimum five years in youth work.

*Training:* Graduate of standard theological seminary.

*Theology:* Committed to the Westminster Standards of the reformed faith with beliefs that are reformed and Presbyterian.

*Attributes:* Must have ability to administer his job and himself.

Must have strong organizational skills.

Must have the education and gifts for counseling the young people of our church.

Must be self-motivated in establishing programs to benefit our youths in areas other than Sunday school. (For example: programs for our outreach in Greenville, in our church, with our children from single-parent homes, for our Covenant children, and with problems that occur with new members.)

Must have a genuine love for kids.

MUST BE A SPIRITUAL GROWTH LEADER WITH A PLAN.

Must be a team player with team-oriented goals working for the good of all areas of our church.

Use this profile as a model, but remember: *every Search Committee should design the profile that uniquely fits the church situation.* The questions discussed in the following chapters are designed to define the answers that should appear on the final product of the profile sheet.

## Chapter 9

# Where Are We Now and Where Do We Want the Youth Ministry to Go?

Several years ago, our church began to realize that youth ministry in the nineties would be different from anything we had ever experienced before. The youth ministry was in transition as we saw a need for increased outreach to young people and families who were emotionally scarred by dysfunctional relationships, unrealistic expectations, and a multitude of external pressures.

At about the same time, the leadership in the

youth ministry was in transition. Our youth pastor accepted a call to another church, and we were looking for new direction in the youth ministry. The Christian education department and our elders commissioned a Youth Pastor Search Committee to find the needed leader, but the committee made a *very* strategic decision early in the process.

Instead of rushing immediately into a search for a new youth pastor, the committee decided to go slowly, review past strengths and weaknesses, formulate the vision for the youth ministry, and then look for a candidate who would be part of fulfilling the church's vision for youths.

After almost eight months of work, the result was the eight-page document "Grace Chapel Youth Ministry—A Vision." The paper was formulated without any particular youth worker in mind (although previous youth workers were consulted for input). The paper included these elements:

- A statement of the *purpose* of the youth ministry. Why are we as a church dedicating ourselves to youth ministry?
- A clarification of the *vision* of the youth ministry. What is the process of developing youths as disciples of Christ that we will undertake?
- An *outline* of our youths and their environment. Our Youth Pastor Search Committee was convinced that the advice of books and articles on youth culture and sociology had to be filtered through the screen of how the students in our area looked in contrast to these findings?

- A series of *recommendations* for the church leaders.
  a) *Staffing.* The committee made the observations that led to the hiring of a full-time junior high pastor.
  b) *Facilities.* The committee recommended that a place be set aside as the official youth "location" in the church (it was not a new idea, but one that our church had neglected for many years).
  c) *Outreach.* The committee recommended a series of church-sponsored youth events designed for evangelistic outreach.
  d) *Incorporation into the body.* The committee saw that youths were marginalized in the church at large, so it suggested better ways to involve them in the life of the whole church.
  e) *Leadership development.* Committee members built a foundation for developing students through discipleship groups and missions teams.
  f) *Budget.* The committee emphasized again that youth ministry's priority in church life is reflected by the budget.

In the midst of this evaluation process, people grew impatient. Students wondered when their new pastor would arrive. We lost some students because the youth ministry could not function at its previous level of activity without full-time leadership.

But hindsight has taught us that the wait was worth it. Many suggestions of the Youth Pastor Search Committee have already been implemented. The current youth pastors (we now have two) are able to refer to this paper and remind church leaders, "We are not introducing something new; we are simply trying to fulfill the vision for youth ministry that you approved *before* we came."

## *What Is the Church's Vision?*

Establishing a sense of the churchwide vision for ministry will simplify the search process. It is much easier to find a person to build the youth ministry within the church's overall vision than it is to ask a youth pastor to undertake the ministry without much idea of what he is working toward. If the youth pastor has no sense of where youth ministry fits in the overall vision of the church, she will either flounder without direction or create a parachurch youth ministry within the church. Having no idea of where youth ministry fits in the big picture of the church invites either conflict or potential failure.

So what does the Search Committee (working in conjunction with church leaders) need to think about with respect to vision?

**Consider the past.** The Search Committee may want to refer to chapter 3 at this point. Understanding the past and present condition of the youth ministry also builds the foundation for asking some of the questions in the other chapters in Part 4. An understanding of past strengths, for example, enables the committee to determine the nonnegotiables (i.e., the areas where the youth pastor *must* be strong).

Evaluating the past and present condition of the youth ministry allows the Search Committee to proceed to issues of the future and to ask, Who is the candidate to move us from where we are to where we'd like to be?

**Dream toward the future.** A vision paper (like the one our Search Committee did) answers, What do we want the youth ministry to look like after this youth pastor is with us five years? As the Search Committee works in partnership with pastoral and lay leaders to dream, the church develops a greater interest in and ownership of the youth ministry. The new youth pastor will feel a church-wide sense of support because the Search Committee has enlarged the church's vision.

One youth pastor advises the Search Committee to "think through [the church's] philosophy of youth ministry. What are you looking for a candidate to produce? Are you program-oriented? People-oriented? What is your priority? To be biblical? Relational? An outreach to the disinterested and hurting? Disciple the few? Develop student leaders? Decide this *before* you settle on your final candidates."

Dreams for the youth ministry future might include some of the categories our Search Committee developed: staffing, facilities, and budget. This vision can also identify dreams that indicate the type of youth pastor the church needs. These dreams might take the following factors into account.

*Size.* Would the church like to see the youth ministry expand numerically? If the answer is yes, the Search Committee may want to include abilities related to this goal (perhaps speaking, organizing, or evangelism) to the profile list.

*Community impact.* Is there a dream for a church youth ministry that will affect junior and senior high schools in the area or respond to specific needs in the region? If this is true, a youth worker experienced with on-campus ministry might be desirable.

One church defined community impact as the primary vision for youth ministry. As a result, the congregation decided to share a staff person with the local Youth for Christ ministry. The arrangement benefited the Youth for Christ worker because it provided office space, 50 percent of his financial support, and a church base. It also benefited the church because members drew upon Youth for Christ's evangelistic experience, and the special arrangement cost them much less.

*Family ministry.* Does the church want someone who can provide ministry to parents? Would the best youth worker have counseling and family therapy experience?

*Volunteers.* Does the church desire to see many of the laity challenged and mobilized for youth ministry? If so, the Youth Pastor Profile should include such abilities. Wayne Rice of Youth Specialties Ministries advises the Search Committee, "Do you have adults in your church who need to be more involved in ministry? Maybe you should look for an older, more experienced youth minister who is good with adults and good at equipping people."

## *Thinking Ahead*

In his popular book *The Seven Habits of Highly Effective People*, Stephen Covey identifies "begin with the end in mind" as one of the seven habits.[1] Covey asserts that the most successful people look ahead, decide where they would like to end up, and then decide on a course of action that will get them there.

Wayne Gretzky, regarded by most sports commentators as one of the greatest hockey players of all time, states this concept in a different way. The secret to his greatness, he says, is that "I skate to where the puck is going to be, not where the puck is."

At this stage in the search process, looking ahead is strategically important. As the profile of the potential youth pastor is developed, the Search Committee must look at the future as well as the present. Look ahead to where the youths and the church are going to be, not just where they are. Begin with the end in mind.

## NOTE

**1.** Stephen Covey, *The Seven Habits of Highly Effective People* (New York: Simon and Schuster, 1989), p. 95ff.

## Chapter 10

# What Does Our Youth Pastor's Resume Look Like?

The issue of a professional resume usually does not come immediately to mind when one thinks of searching for a youth pastor. Many consider love for teenagers or relational ability as the absolute essentials, with college education, experience in youth work, and potential theological education as nice additions.

Experts in the youth ministry field, however, generally agree that someone who depends on relational charisma or love for kids *alone* will not be able to respond to the complexities of the nineties. We need youth workers who are trained to address theological issues (e.g., addressing the gospel to a pluralistic society) and moral issues (e.g., addressing AIDS, abortion, and sexual promiscuity).

Today, churches that understand the rigors of reaching young people usually use words like *experienced*, *trained*, or *professional* in their descriptions of the youth workers they need.

In the formation of this Youth Pastor Profile, the Search Committee must ask, What previous experiences and/or education should appear on the candidate's resume?

## *Three Areas to Consider*

God reminded Samuel in the selection of King David that human beings focus on the "outward appearance" while God "looks at the heart" (1 Sam. 16:7). Some will read into this verse an aversion to considering the outward appearance qualifications that appear on a resume, but the Search Committee must look at both. The resume will explain something about outward appearance preparedness; the interview process will offer an opportunity to respond to the candidate's heart.

When developing the Youth Pastor Profile, the Search Committee should give special consideration to three areas in evaluating resumes.

**1. Education.** Is the church looking for a Bible school graduate? Is a seminary education, with the possibility of ordination to the ministry, important? If the candidate has a nonreligious degree, should it be in sociology or adolescent psychology? Will the focus be specifically on Christian college graduates who majored in youth ministry?

The educational requirements vary widely according to church tradition, denominational standards, and the desired priorities of the youth ministry. In every case, the educational background may hint at the strengths of a youth pastor.

In our church, I became the youth pastor after completing my undergraduate degree in business administration and management. I was a seminary student at the time, working to complete my Master of Divinity degree. Under my leadership, the programming was strong; I organized great retreats and multiple summer mission teams. My administrative gifts and training benefited the youth ministry.

Another youth pastor who followed me had an undergraduate degree in sociology and a Master of Divinity degree. He understood youth culture. The youth group benefited because he was able to explain how the gospel applied to the youth culture of the day. He used his training in sociology as I had used my training in administration.

An academic factor to consider pertains to the church's perspective on ordination. If the youth pastor must be ordained to maintain the long-term respect of the church as a "real" minister, the academic training that the church associates with ordination takes on greater significance. Having an ordained youth pastor is often one principal way a church can express the priority and significance of the youth ministry.

The information in chapter 11, "Where *Must* Our Youth Pastor Be Strong?" should help the Search Committee determine the specific types of academic background required to fit the desired Youth Pastor Profile.

**2. Youth ministry experience.** One Search Committee humorously described the ideal youth pastor as a twenty-five-year-old with lots of energy and fifteen years of proven youth ministry service. The description strikes at several significant issues related to youth ministry experience. A younger youth leader may have lots of energy but no idea of how to direct it: zeal without knowledge. A veteran of thirty years in youth work may be as wise as Solomon but too worn out to start in a new position.

So what does the church want—a novice or a veteran? A large church with a large pool of volunteers and some paid youth ministry interns may desire someone with five or more years of experience, which will be needed to lead the team, direct the energy of the part-timers, and train the staff. In this case, supervisory experience and the ability to lead others in youth ministry may be considered more important than direct ministry with students.

On the other hand, a smaller church may be willing to hire a novice with the potential for growth. Energy and willingness to cultivate relationships with teenagers might be the priority, so the church may be content to accept a younger, less-experienced candidate who will learn by doing.

Other factors to consider under experience include service in a parachurch youth ministry. A person with great expertise based on twelve years with Campus Crusade or Young Life may seem to be an ideal candidate, but will that candidate have the patience needed to deal with the red tape of life in the local church? (Refer to chapter 5, "Do We Understand the Philosophy of Church Youth Ministry?" for more detail on this matter.)

Experience also answers other questions. What kind of spiritual gifts have been demonstrated and cultivated? If teaching and administration are priority requirements, the resume should reflect them. What has been the past youth group size? The transition from a group of twenty to a group of fifty can overwhelm a youth pastor with administration and details. Does other experience indicate that the candidate could make such a transition?

**3. Personal mission statement.** At some point on the resume, a candidate usually provides a personal purpose or mission statement. It often includes a statement of a long-term goal, and it reflects the individual's career vision.

This personal mission statement indicates the candidate's long-term commitment to youth ministry. What should the Search Committee be looking for?

Some leaders in the field of youth ministry insist that the best youth workers have a career or lifetime commitment to youth ministry. If this is a requirement of the Search Committee, it should be reflected in the Youth Pastor Profile.

Others advise that a long-term youth ministry commitment of five years is more than adequate for most churches. The changing nature of adolescent life-styles and issues combined with the other changes in the life of the youth worker should allow the youth pastor to make periodic reevaluations. Thus, a lifetime commitment is perhaps too much to expect.

## *Two Areas to Remain Open About*

A Search Committee will be tempted to rule out candidates based on marital status or age, but it shouldn't. Persons of various ages and marital statuses make good youth pastors.

**Marital status.** Youth pastors fall into several categories, any of which have their respective pros.

*The single youth pastor* often has lots of time and loads of energy to offer the youth group.

The youth pastor who is *married without kids* (or the older youth worker with grown children) can also offer enormous amounts of time to the youth ministry.

The *family-oriented youth pastor*, with two or three small children at home, can provide a great model of family relationships to the youths. The youth pastor can allow students to share in the family life and participate in the care for the children.

**Age.** Being young is not a requirement for effective youth ministry. Some of the most effective youth communicators of our time are men and women in their forties and fifties. One sixty-year-old youth pastor leads a ministry that includes his grandchildren. In a time when students desperately need youth leaders who will act as surrogate parents, older youth workers are more needed than ever before.

Age is like marital status; each category has pros. The experienced veteran may know practically everything about young people and need little supervision. A novice may earn immediate credibility with students and can probably be effectively developed as she grows.

## *Connect the Dots*

A Search Committee should never regard the resume as the complete picture, but it provides a rough outline enabling the committee to decide whether to pursue the candidate any further.

When formulating the Youth Pastor Profile, the Search Committee should view the elements of the resume as guidelines, which create, in effect, the dots, which must be connected to complete the outline of the desired youth pastor. The additional information accumulated through questionnaires, interviews, and references will complete the picture.

## Chapter 11

# Where *Must* Our Youth Pastor Be Strong?

**W**hat are some of the jobs a youth pastor will be expected to fulfill? To all, he will be a spiritual example who will be examined in the depth of his relationship with God as well as the health of his primary relationships. To some students, the youth pastor may be a coach, mentor, or surrogate parent. To others, she may be a programmer or an administrator. To the church, he may be the trainer of adults or the discipler of the future of the church.

But only Jesus did all things well. The rest of us—including the desired youth pastor—have strengths and weaknesses. What does the Search

Committee pinpoint as the absolute essentials for the youth pastor? Pat MacMillan puts it this way: "What must this person accomplish in order to get an excellent evaluation from me?"[1]

## *Three Absolutes*

Qualities of the youth pastor's ministry will not necessarily be synonymous with the job description the youth pastor is asked to fulfill. As a result, several qualities demand attention at the outset.

Charles Smith, a veteran of over twenty years of directing Christian education ministry, urges Youth Pastor Search Committees to consider three overarching issues as absolutes for any potential youth ministry candidate.

**1. Is the candidate theologically consistent?** Young people are confused enough about the nature of God and the nature of Christian living. They need a leader who demonstrates consistency and conviction in the way he lives out Christian commitment.

**2. Does the candidate relate well to young people?** Although the ability to cultivate volunteers is crucial to effective youth ministry, the youth pastor will lead primarily by example. If she knows how to care for, reach out to, and disciple students, the other leaders in the youth ministry are able to follow.

**3. Does the candidate know how to use a staff?** Is the candidate a one-person show, or is the person secure enough to lead the youth ministry through a team? The loner will not survive the youth ministry of the nineties; too many students need intensive care from adult leaders.

## *Job Descriptions*

Qualities provide the foundation for effective ministry, but a job description defines the structure of the job. The job description can always be modified according to the skills and ministry strengths that develop over time, but the youth ministry candidate should be able to look at the basic job description and say, "These are the foundation points of this church's youth ministry. If I cannot fulfill these basic requirements, the job is not for me."

This question addresses the issue of expectations. Speaking again to that topic, veteran youth worker Tom McLaughlin advises Search Committees to separate their expectations into categories of negotiable and nonnegotiable: "It may not be as important to you that your youth pastor be married or have experience leading foreign mission teams. These might be negotiable issues. However, it may be very important that the person have a clear vision for youth ministry or a heart for leading youths to Christ. These then become identified as your nonnegotiable expectations."

Grace Chapel high school minister Mike Allen

advises Search Committees, *"Be specific in your expectations.* How many hours work per week will the church expect? How many days off? What programs should be started? Which existing programs should be continued? How much freedom will be given to initiate new ideas? Will he or she be supported with adult volunteers? With office space? With secretarial help? With a computer? Will the youth pastor be considered a 'real' pastor? What other pastoral responsibilities will be expected—pastoral counseling, hospital visitation, etc.?"

Mike goes on to recommend that these expectations be spelled out in a detailed job description, outlining the tasks necessary to do youth ministry: "Don't assume anything. Think through every possibility and be clear about what you expect." (Sample job descriptions are included in Appendix D.)

Scanning through various books on basic youth ministry can help the Search Committee identify reasonable expectations in the church youth ministry. The categories listed in these books give an overview of all of the potential facets of youth ministry that a youth pastor might fulfill.

In *The Youth Builder*, for example, Jim Burns lists ten aspects of practical strategy for youth ministry, which accurately depict the most basic jobs churches assign to the youth pastor:

1. Discipleship—getting kids involved
2. Relational evangelism
3. Getting kids excited about missions and service

4. Camps and retreats
5. Worship
6. Developing student leadership
7. Building community through small groups
8. Developing dynamic adult volunteers
9. Building support with your pastor, staff, and church
10. Coping with finances[2]

Any one of these could be the focal strength of our youth pastor, but where *must* our candidate be strong? Search Committee members seek to answer this question as they continue to formulate the Youth Pastor Profile.

## *The Custom-Made Youth Pastor*

Deciding the specifics of the youth pastor will influence the long-term success of the youth program. Mike Allen observes, "Like it or not, the shape of the youth ministry will be directly related to the personality of the youth pastor. And the longer a youth pastor is there, the more like him the ministry will become—no matter how many volunteers are involved. Search Committee members need to decide if they are looking for a 'status quo' youth minister or a visionary; and if they choose a visionary, they must be willing to give that visionary the needed freedom to change, add, or delete programs."

Determining where the youth pastor must be

strong reminds the Search Committee that every church is unique. The Youth Pastor Profile for every church should reflect the character of that church as well as the leadership's long-term hopes for the youth program.

A musically inclined church may want someone who can lead young people in effective worship. A church built on small group ministry will want a youth minister with experience in that area who can incorporate students into small groups. Our church invests heavily in cross-cultural missions so we sought a youth minister who could motivate our high schoolers for missions and service.

Although some youth programs exist virtually autonomously from the rest of the church, most youth ministries tend to reflect the unique nature of the church out of which they come. So again, the Search Committee should ask, What model of youth ministry best fits our church? Is it a discipling ministry? A friendship evangelism outreach to unchurched kids? A caring ministry to dysfunctional kids and their families? A multiple-option ministry (where kids always have something to go to or choose from)?

And which model of youth pastor is the church's priority? A *pastor* who shepherds the youth congregation? A *coach* who emphasizes training for ministry? A *programmer* who creates a full-service youth ministry? A *counselor* who bandages the wounded? Does *musical ability* or *athletic prowess* matter?

In formulating a Youth Pastor Profile and an

accompanying job description, the Search Committee must decide which type of ministry and styles of leadership best fit the church's desired youth ministry goals. Then the committee can enter into wish listing—the topic of the next chapter.

## NOTES

1. Pat MacMillan, *Hiring Excellence* (Colorado Springs: NavPress, 1992), p. 74.

2. Jim Burns, *The Youth Builder* (Eugene, Oreg.: Harvest House, 1988), pp. 61–167.

## Chapter 12

# If We Could Paint Our Ideal, We'd Also Like...

The preceding chapter focused on the bare essentials that the youth pastor candidate should demonstrate, but the Search Committee should also take an opportunity to dream. What gifts, skills, and experience would the committee like to see in addition to the required minimum? Should the candidate demonstrate ability to work with groups like Pioneer Girls, Brigade, or Awana Clubs? Should he be able to preach occasionally? Is experience coordinating outreach concerts desirable? Is the administrative know-how for organizing cross-cultural mission teams part of the wish list? If the candidate is gifted in music or in drama, would that imply a hope that she will coordinate choir tours, puppet ministry, or drama teams?

## *Categories*

In the previous chapter, we identified some absolutes for the youth pastor. Now we explore the it-sure-would-be-nice categories.

As the profile formation continues, the Search Committee can discuss all of these categories and then assign priorities to them.

**Counseling.** Although basic counseling is a necessity for most youth ministry, some churches would genuinely appreciate a youth pastor who can do family counseling, crisis management, or even therapy. These are special skills.

**Evangelistic or on-campus experience.** Most churches would like to see their youth ministry increase outreach to local campuses, but is this a ministry that can be developed or does it need to be something that the candidate can do upon arrival? If there is an immediate desire to intensify this aspect of the ministry, Search Committees should look on the resume for experience in evangelistic training, junior or senior high teaching, coaching, or parachurch ministry.

**Extraordinary administrative abilities.** Every youth pastor should be expected to coordinate the basic program, the volunteers, and the youth budget, but some churches aspire for youth programs that demand unusual administrative strengths. A church's desire for massive outreach campaigns, multiple mission teams, or church-sponsored youth concerts means that the Search Committee should be praying and looking for someone with above-minimum management skills.

**Extraordinary communication skills.** Ability to communicate with young people is a basic foundation for the youth pastor, but if she will be expected to preach monthly to the whole congregation, lead seminars for parents, or teach a course at a local school, the Search Committee's expectation list should reflect this (and the candidate should probably demonstrate ability in one of these areas during a candidating visit).

**Intervention ministry.** Are there quite a few students in the group with major problems—psychologically, academically, or legally? If the youth pastor will need to spend large amounts of energy involved in intervention ministry with local counselors, the schools, or parole boards, he should probably have demonstrated some experience in these areas.

**Cross-cultural ability.** Churches across America are becoming increasingly multicultural. As a result, youth pastors need some of the gifts once associated with missionaries—able to bridge the gap between multiple cultures.

**Creative ministry.** This category includes some of the ministries mentioned earlier—puppet ministry, drama, and music. But it also includes skills that today's youth pastor might need in teaching or communication. Does the youth pastor need to know how to produce videos—either for teaching or simply for youth group fun? Will she be expected to produce a monthly newsletter that will require the use of computer-generated graphics? Will the youth minister be asked to create multiscreen slide shows?

## *Reality Check*

Another church wrote to me with their Youth Pastor Profile. It was five single-spaced pages. A week later, they called for my feedback. I offered them the same response that I had hesitated to give another church a few years earlier.

"It looks great," I said, "but I have one question: How many people are you looking for to fill this position?" It was my not-so-gentle way of telling them that their profile was unrealistic.

As the Youth Pastor Profile is formulated, the Search Committee must periodically review whether or not the hopes reflected in it are realistic. Jesus, the Messiah, sits on the right hand of God in heaven; He will not be a candidate. Superman is not a candidate, either; at this writing, he is dead.

So who is the person the committee is looking for? Perhaps it is time to review the sample profile at the beginning of Part 4 to make sure that the committee's expectations are within the realm of reality.

## Chapter 13

# What Are We Willing to Pay for Our Youth Ministry?

One discount clothing outlet advertises itself as the store where you get maximum value for minimum cost. Is this the perspective of your church toward the youth ministry? Is your church investing in youth ministry (and therefore in the best possible youth minister), or is it trying to get the maximum for the minimum?

Jim Tonkowich served with FOCUS, a ministry to prep school students. He urges churches regarding youth ministers: "Be willing to pay the freight. Churches give a good deal of lip service to the importance of youth work. In my experience, nearly 80 percent of the followers of Christ first came to faith before they turned twenty-one. Yet the sad fact is that this is not reflected in the youth ministry budget or the youth minister's salary. Churches need to exercise more faith than to offer less than living wage in hope of getting someone who will be able to live above a member's garage or whose spouse will make up the difference. If it is important to have a youth minister, it is important to pay him or her adequately."

No issue gets hotter responses from youth pastors than this issue of salary. One youth pastor told me of getting to the final candidating process before the details of salary were discussed. He had taken what he thought was the most spiritual approach: determine if he were called to the church and then trust God for the salary.

He and his wife thought that the church was a real fit with their gifts and abilities. The students responded well in initial meetings. Parents seemed receptive. But when the salary package was revealed, the youth pastor realized that he could not care for his family unless his wife worked full-time outside the home. After that news, he struggled to determine God's call in the midst of his confusion.

Wayne Rice, youth ministry expert and cofounder of Youth Specialties Ministries, encourages churches, "Provide decent salaries for your youth ministers. Don't handicap them by making them moonlight or run from creditors all the time." Wayne meets hundreds of youth leaders every year, and he knows the pain that many underpaid youth pastors work under as they try to serve God and live within the salaries they have been given.

A survey by Dr. Mark Lamport of Gordon College's youth ministry department revealed that salary was one of the top three reasons why youth workers would consider leaving the ministry or their current position.[1]

The salary issue touches upon the bigger topic of the compensation of all persons in ministry. In general, however, every pastor's salary and benefits package (including the youth pastor's) ought to take into account several realities.

## Economic Realities

The high turnover rate in youth leaders (some have estimated a turnover rate as high as once every two years) is sometimes caused by the economic realities that drive them into other careers or ministries. In shaping the economic package, the Search Committee needs to ask a number of questions.

**Adequacy.** Will the salary offered enable the youth pastor to obtain adequate housing, live at a level roughly equivalent to the average church member, and feed the family without using food stamps?

**Allowances.** If the denomination sets the salary and benefits standard, are allowances made to help those who accept jobs in the more expensive parts of the country?

**Privacy.** If the youth pastor lives in a church-owned apartment or parsonage, will there be any opportunity for family privacy? (One youth pastor found out after he was hired that he was also the unofficial caretaker of the church building because his parsonage was on the church property.) *Corollary*: if the church-provided housing does not permit much privacy, can the salary be increased to encourage quarterly vacation getaways for the youth minister and family?

**Equity.** Will there be an opportunity to gain any equity? In other words, will the church entertain helping the youth pastor purchase housing? In a day when most house prices are still far beyond the range of first-time buyers, an equity-sharing plan for pastors is a very attractive part of a salary package. (In contrast, inability to purchase housing often drives the thirty-something youth pastor to pursue youth ministry in a less expensive area.)

**Advancement.** Are there opportunities for economic advancement within the youth ministry position, or must the youth pastor consider another ministry to get a significant raise? Some churches have an unstated policy that keeps youth pastors poor until they aspire to be "real" pastors (the ones who preach).

Mike Allen, our high school pastor at Grace

Chapel, summarizes the economic expectations that the best youth workers will bring to a church: "Although you don't always just 'get what you pay for' (you might get more than you pay for), you definitely only 'keep what you pay for.' Don't just pay enough to hire a youth pastor. Pay enough to keep the person for the long haul. Longevity in youth ministry is very important. Include a plan for adequate raises and a fair compensation package of health and life insurance as well as retirement. Pay for the move. It would also help to have a clear-cut and consistent housing policy (will the church help with down payments?). Take into consideration the youth pastor's family as well. And then, on top of salary, provide the youth pastor with a budget adequate for curriculum, trip scholarships, professional development, and other youth ministry costs."

## *Comparative Realities*

We all would like to think that the youth minister we hire will commit his salary to the Lord in prayer and never wonder about what anyone else on the staff or in the church gets paid. Given the human condition, however, we would best assume that he will make some comparisons. In this respect, the Search Committee needs to ask more questions.

**Other pastors.** What will the youth pastor make in comparison to other pastors on staff? This is especially significant in churches where the pastors' salaries are public knowledge. If the youth pastor candidate is thirty-four, is committed to youth ministry for the long term, has an advanced degree (Master of Divinity or M.A. in theology, for example), and brings eight years of experience to the ministry, how will she be compensated in contrast to an associate pastor who is thirty-two? How will the youth pastor's package compare to other pastors with less education or experience?

One church resolved this issue by creating levels of staffing—all of which were subject to the same pay scales. With a structure similar to a university system, they identified assistant pastors, associate pastors, and the senior pastor. The Personnel Committee established a pay scale for each level based on seniority, experience, and job responsibility so that an assistant in pastoral care would make less than an associate in youth ministry.

Within this structure, a youth worker was given opportunities to advance economically without feeling forced to leave the youth ministry. The system also affirmed the youth minister's stature as a "real" pastor and as a full member of the ministerial team.

**Church members.** What will the youth minister make in comparison to the average church member? One youth worker told me that she could not afford to dress as nicely as the students in her ministry (a *very* significant factor in a ministry where young people are often superconscious of attire and looks). In communities where most of the mothers work outside the home, perhaps the youth pastor's spouse should be expected to do the same, but if most church families have stay-at-home moms, the youth pastor should be compensated enough to live at an equal level.

**Other professionals.** How will the youth professional's salary compare to the annual salaries of those with similar occupations in the community (teachers, school administrators, coaches, counselors, etc.)?

## Growth Opportunities

If the Search Committee desires a youth pastor who will be a growing person, will the salary package allow for conferences, seminars, and books?

One long-term youth pastor challenged our church when he told us that his most valued benefit was the $1,500 his church allocated every year for his personal growth as a youth ministry professional. He could use the money to attend a conference, pursue course work toward another degree, or purchase youth ministry-related resources. In his tenure at his church, he earned a doctorate in ministry, focusing on the topic of training youths to do evangelism.

## Benefits

Health insurance, life insurance, retirement plans, and vacations factor into the overall plan.

One church offered free tuition for the youth pastor's children at the Christian academy associated with the school. Since that youth pastor had four children, it was a *significant* benefit.

In many jobs, the benefit package might cost as much as 30 percent of the salary, yet it is a factor that can help a potential youth ministry candidate say yes. The Search Committee (or the committee that determines salary) needs to determine what benefits will provide the candidate with adequate coverage.

## The Rest of the Budget

Wayne Rice writes again, "Make sure to provide an adequate youth budget, over and above salary, for resources, activities, office help, etc." Even when a salary is adequate, the youth minister may be strapped if there is not a reasonable budget to support a growing ministry.

Such a budget will vary widely in each church. Consult Appendix H on youth ministry budgeting for ideas. A Search Committee that prepares an adequate youth budget, which is in place when the new youth pastor arrives, can save the person an enormous amount of frustration in the early months of ministry.

## The Priority Issue Again

The real question with respect to finances involves priorities: Where does youth ministry fit in the church's overall sense of mission? Veteran youth leader Dawson McAllister summarizes the issue: "Give youth ministry financial priority. The average youth budget in one denomination is just 4 percent of its budget. If giving to missions is a high priority, consider that one of our ripest mission fields is youth."[2]

## NOTES

1. Eugene C. Roehlkepartain, ed., *The Youth Ministry Resource Book* (Loveland, Colo.: GROUP Books, 1988), p. 189.

2. Dawson McAllister, "Reaching Teens: What a Church Can Do," *Moody Monthly*, March 1992, p. 22.

## Chapter 14

# Where Do We Get Contacts?

The Youth Pastor Profile is nearing completion, but where does the Search Committee start to look for the person who can fill this position? No matter how thorough the work of the Search Committee, the success of the process still depends on being put in touch with effective candidates. This is one of the tougher parts of the search because most Search Committee members do not have a network into which to tap for contacts.

Before highlighting some contact networks, I offer one word of caution for the Search Committee: the person who is aggressively looking for a ministry change may not be the most suitable contact. Though many youth workers speak of a "restless-

115

ness for a new challenge" that may precede a job change, the person who is actively searching for a change may be indicating that he is looking for greener grass or she is running from an uncomfortable ministry situation.

The best way to avoid this problem when using these networks is to ask, "Do you know of anyone successfully engaged in youth ministry we could contact to see if that person would be willing to talk with us?" A question phrased in this way will get far better results than asking, "Do you know of anyone looking for a job in youth ministry?"

## *The Networks*

In addition to the networks cited below, individuals who train youth workers are listed in Appendix F, "Personal Contacts." Here are some of the avenues a Search Committee might consider (outside word of mouth, which is still the principal tool used by many Search Committees).

**The denominational network.** A church that maintains a tight denominational tie will benefit from a discussion with the denomination's national office, especially if there is a national office dedicated to youth ministry. The Assemblies of God, Southern Baptists, Nazarenes, Christian and Missionary Alliance, and Evangelical Free Church are a few examples of denominations with national youth ministry offices and often national youth workers.

These offices can recommend youth workers within the church's tradition who might be willing to consider a contact from the Search Committee. These national offices host national or regional get-togethers of youth workers where job opportunities are often shared.

Contacting the denominational headquarters can often add another benefit. The national youth minister can offer feedback on the job description (or the Youth Pastor Profile) that the Search Committee prepares, the anticipated salary structure, and the goals for the youth ministry position. This feedback can help the Search Committee compare itself against other churches in similar situations.

**Bible schools and Christian colleges.** Numerous Christian schools now offer youth ministry as a major. Contacting the placement office or the youth ministry professors at these schools can lead the Search Committee to promising graduates or alumni.

Obviously, there could be some difficulty in some churches in hiring a youth minister who is only twenty-one or twenty-two years old, but many youth ministry majors are older students who have returned to school for the specific reason of going into youth work.

**Seminaries.** The Search Committee probably does not want a seminarian who is graduating, desperate for work, and willing to entertain any job—even youth ministry! But many in seminary have pursued graduate degrees and desire to go into long-term youth ministry as professional, ordained youth ministers.

The best way to find these students is through the alumni office, the placement office, or—if possible—a personal visit to the seminary.

**Other youth workers.** Any youth worker who has been at it for more than three or four years usually has a network. Contacting youth workers in the area or the denomination can lead to positive prospects to meet the church's needs.

If the church had an outgoing youth pastor (and if that youth pastor departed under relatively favorable conditions), the person might be a great source for contacts because of the knowledge of the church's needs as well as the culture of the church and the region.

**Youth worker networks.** Various informal nationwide networks provide opportunity for youth workers to interact. The Search Committee can take advantage of these networks when looking for a youth pastor.

*Youth Specialties. Youthworker Update,* a monthly newsletter, includes a special service that connects churches searching for a youth pastor with youth workers looking for a change. *The National Youth Workers Convention* draws over fifteen hundred youth workers for a four-day conference, and the convention headquarters includes a networking station where churches can connect with potential candidates. *The Youth Specialties One-Day Seminar* occurs in over three hundred locations across the country.

Contact: Youth Specialties Ministries, 1224 Greenfield Drive, El Cajon, California 92021; 619-440-2333.

*GROUP.* This organization has a vast array of youth worker contacts through magazines and publications. It also hosts the *Youth Ministry University*, which draws men and women with a long-term commitment to youth ministry.

Contact: *GROUP*, P.O. Box 481, Loveland, Colorado 80539; 303-669-3836.

*Leadership Forum.* This group hosts an annual get-together of youth leaders from some of the nation's largest and most prominent churches. Contacting these individuals can get the Search Committee's needs out to some of our country's best networked youth specialists who can then provide references.

Contact: Fred Smith, Leadership Network, P.O. Box 9100, Tyler, Texas 75711-9100; 903-561-0437.

*Local and regional networks.* Many youth workers are tied together through the *National Network of Youth Ministries* and participate in local or regional youth worker events. These events are some of the best opportunities to meet local youth leaders who might be a smooth cultural fit with the church.

Contact: The National Network of Youth Ministries, 17150 Via del Campo, Suite 102, San Diego, California 92127; 619-451-1111.

*Parachurch youth ministries.* Young Life, Youth for Christ, or Campus Crusade's Student Venture can often be a great contact.

Contact:

National Institute of Youth Ministry, 940 Calle Amanecer, Suite G, San Clemente, California 92672; 714-498-4418.

Student Venture, c/o Campus Crusade for Christ, 100 Sunport Lane, Orlando, Florida 32809; 407-826-2000.

Young Life, P.O. Box 520, Colorado Springs, Colorado 80901; 719-473-4262.

Youth for Christ USA, P.O. Box 228822, Denver, Colorado 80222; 303-843-9000.

Youth Leadership, 122 West Franklin Avenue, Suite 210, Minneapolis, Minnesota 55404; 612-870-3632.

## *As the Search Committee Makes Contact*

In the process of generating the contact list, the Search Committee should remember several steps that can contribute to overall success.

**Have materials ready.** Although the Search Committee may want to start gathering names to consider as soon as the committee is formed, a specific search should not go forward aggressively until these materials are ready to send to prospective candidates:

- A preliminary candidate questionnaire
- A Youth Pastor Profile
- A potential job description
- A profile of and statement of faith from the church

**Be direct.** Boldly contact someone being considered as a candidate. Do not say, "We're looking for a youth pastor, and we're wondering if you have anyone to suggest," while hoping that the person will suggest herself. When asking for references, do so directly.

**But don't promise too much.** Ask someone if he would be willing to enter into preliminary dialogue with the Search Committee. Some Search Committees ask potential candidates to pray about whether they would be willing to enter into the process. If the committee is speaking to a number of candidates, advise each one of that fact. The caution—especially at the outset—is to avoid sending signals that imply a greater commitment than the Search Committee has.

**And keep it a secret.** Discretion will serve both the church and the potential candidate. Hinting at the potential candidate too early can cause unnecessary reaction (either positive anticipation or negative reaction) in the church. It can also cause the candidate to lose credibility at the present work site if people hear that a change may be forthcoming.

*Part 5*

# The Interview Process

## Chapter 15

# What to Look for in the Interview Process

A profile has been created. Initial contacts are established. Now it is time to explore the potential candidates. This can be the most frightening part of the process because the Search Committee will always wonder, Will any person actually come close to fitting our profile? or How can we tell if we have the right person?

### *Before the Official Interview*

The search process requires much work *before* the candidate appears at the church for an interview. Several actions on behalf of the Search Committee will determine if a candidate should be pursued.

**Informational forms.** Application forms and more detailed questionnaires can screen the candidates quite effectively. Sample forms and questions are found in the Appendixes.

When circulating these forms, the Search Committee should

- ask the candidates to type answers so that the responses can be photocopied to the entire committee.
- establish a deadline: "If you are interested in talking with us about this position, please return this to us by June 1."
- assure the potential candidate of confidentiality. Send the forms to the home address. One church established a special post office box to receive replies so that the responses were not being circulated through the church office.

**The resume.** Pat MacMillan, in *Hiring Excellence*, offers a fine checklist of what a Search Committee should look for in evaluating a candidate's resume.

*Achievement.* "Look for specific instances of goal accomplishment, the ability to bring a project from concept to completion."

*Growth and progress.* "Look for growth in skills and responsibilities."

*Clear thinking and communication.* Is the resume "wordy, stuffed full of adjectives and superlatives, and disorganized? Or is it realistic and clear?"

*Stability.* Beware people who have changed jobs frequently; "look to see if there wasn't at least one job of significant (five years or more) duration."

*Education.* Try to see if there is a match between the person's education and the church's requirements, and beware vague references to education that make the resume appear better than it really is.

*Personal data.* Excessive references to personal data may "indicate lack of focus" or "an attempt to pad the resume here to make up for weaknesses elsewhere."

*Graphics.* "I've often thought there might be an inverse relationship between the quality of the candidate and the glitz or slickness of the resume."[1]

**Telephone interviews.** Modern technology can be a tool to assist in the work of the Search Committee. A conference call (or, in the days ahead, a video conference call) often accomplishes as much as a face-to-face visit, at least in the preliminary stages of the search when the Search Committee is narrowing the field.

Telephone interviews work best when the Search Committee has prepared a basic list of questions beforehand (the committee may want to mail or fax these questions to the interviewees so that they have time to think through answers). If there is a large field of prospective candidates and Search Committee members are interviewing several candidates separately, all should have the same basic list of questions so that the feedback can be evaluated as objectively as possible.

**An interview in the candidate's world.** Perhaps the chairperson of the Search Committee can meet the candidate where he currently lives or serves. This visit can open the door for face-to-face references as well as opportunities to observe the candidate in action with a group of young people with whom he is familiar.

**References.** Past ministry experience foreshadows what the candidate might do in a church. A football coach told his team, "What you do in practice you will do in a game." In other words, no matter how sparkling and impressive a candidate may be in an interview, the church is going to get the person the candidate has been in the past. Of course, all of us grow and develop by God's grace over time, but this process is often slow. Thus, references will provide the best insights about what the candidates are really like in day-to-day situations.

To get the broadest view of the candidate, Steve

Macchia, president of the Evangelistic Association of New England and consultant to hundreds of New England churches, offers the following advice in securing references: "I like to talk with a current peer in ministry, a current supervisor, a mentor or professor, and a colleague in ministry. These reference calls also need to have a consistent group of questions to be covered so that you can compare the responses received."

Len Kageler, youth ministry veteran and author, adds here that "asking references to fill out psychological tests [like the lion-otter-beaver-golden retriever test mentioned on the following page] on behalf of the candidate enables the Search Committee to understand how other people view the candidate."

**Spiritual questions.** If possible, try to discern the candidate's walk with God from people personally associated with her. If the person is not grounded and fairly mature spiritually, he will not stay long and will not have much of a lasting impact. Spiritual integrity is not the only issue, but other qualities cannot produce effective ministry without it.

**Psychological evaluations.** How healthy is the candidate emotionally? If she is typical of our culture's recent dysfunctional offspring, she may have some issues that can affect ministry leadership. The Myers-Briggs test or other such personality inventories, with a trained professional's interpretation of the results, can help the Search Committee understand the candidate better.[2]

Another evaluation system that addresses youth ministry issues specifically is done in association with SonLife Ministries.[3] Their psychological testing identifies youth workers as

- *lions*—strong on up-front leadership, good with large groups, and excellent in providing vision. But lions can ignore some of the neediest people and may be inclined toward dominating behavior.

- *otters*—full of charisma. Otters are the fun-loving, life-of-the-party types; they're great in managing multiple relationships but may have difficulty in going deep enough to counsel. They could be weak on organizing and planning.

- *beavers*—detailed and meticulous in planning. Beavers are good choices if the church wants efficient programs, but they can be boring and ineffective as up-front leaders.

- *golden retrievers*—good in one-on-one relationships. In a crowd, golden retrievers can see one person in great need or pain; they focus on the one and make great counselors. But golden retrievers may not want up-front ministry and may ignore the larger flock in favor of the one lost sheep.

Psychological testing can assist both the Search Committee and the candidate in establishing strengths and weaknesses that will help determine if the church and the candidate fit.

## *After the Forms ... Face-to-Face*

What questions should be asked as the candidate first visits with the Search Committee? How can these questions help determine if there will be a fit of youth minister and church?

Steve Macchia writes, "In hiring any staff person, I try to ask all of the hard questions up front before the interview process goes too far. Some of the hard questions pertain to the following areas: self-assessment; personal and spiritual history; ministry experience and education; spiritual giftedness; personality evaluation. The first stage in the interviewing process is to do a lot of listening. Therefore, you need to have mapped out ahead of time the kinds of questions you'll be asking and then compare these answers between candidates."

Following Macchia's advice, the Search Committee should form provocative, open-ended questions, especially those that address expectations. For example, to find out the greatest convictions of the candidate, ask, "If you had only *one* talk to give to a youth group, what might your topic be?" rather than, "What are your top convictions regarding youth ministry?" The former question allows departure from rehearsed answers into the realm of the candidate's heart.

The following is a list of sample questions that the Search Committee might ask in an interview. Some of them are repetitive with the forms that are completed before the interview process (see the Appendixes), but asking them in person provides a greater opportunity to understand the candidate's full perspective.

- "Why are you applying for this job?" The Search Committee should look for a genuine sense of call to youth ministry.
- "What are your gifts and talents that qualify you for this position?"
- "What can you tell us about your youth ministry experience when you were a teenager?" Remember, many youth workers tend to imitate the ministry they were brought up in.
- "How much formal training have you had in youth ministry?"
- "What type of informal training (an influential mentor, seminars, conferences, personal study projects) have you been involved in?"
- "What is your attitude toward parents?" If the applicant is very young (early twenties), the committee may also want to ask questions about the candidate's relationship with her own parents since that relationship is often projected by young youth leaders onto the parents of the young people in the ministry.
- "How do you plan to involve parents in your youth ministry?" Most experts agree that this is a key component of youth ministry in the nineties. Len Kageler asserts that today's youth ministers must realize that "we are working with 'systems,' not just with youth, and a primary influence in the youth's system is the parents."
- "What are your views on social life and sexuality?" It is a very complicated issue, especially if

the candidate is not married. Some people enter youth ministry to hang around with adolescent girls and boys. A thorough background check is always in order. The Search Committee will not need to look far for stories of youth workers who have hurt young people, churches, and themselves through moral failure within the youth ministry.

- "What are your priorities in your philosophy of youth ministry? Is evangelism important? What can you tell us about the last young person you led to faith? Discipleship? What do your current discipling relationships look like? Mission teams or service opportunities? Where have you been involved?" The key here is that the candidate's greatest strengths be in accordance with the church's greatest expectations.
- "What are you reading for personal growth? What is the last book you read? How did it affect you?" The answers here can give clues into the candidate's personal disciplines and commitment to growth.

Use case studies (Len Kageler also advocates role playing to get an idea of how the candidate relates to people). Observe the candidate's maturity and ability to solve problems appropriately by presenting case studies on real issues he might face: a suicidal teenager, a drug abuse issue, a runaway from a church family, a youth accusing a parent of sexual or physical abuse, and so on.

## *What to Look for: Qualities*

Woody Phillips, former executive pastor of Church of the Savior in Wayne, Pennsylvania, and now overseer of mission work in Eastern Europe, focuses on a variety of qualities in potential missionary candidates. Youth ministry is in itself a cross-cultural ministry where an adult leaves her culture and goes into the culture of a teenager to present Jesus Christ in a way that is culturally relevant and provokes positive change. As a result, Phillips's criteria can be applied to persons considering youth ministry.

**1. A solid walk with Christ, prayer, and Bible study.** Elaborating on this point, Dewey Bertolini, youth ministry professor at the Masters College, writes,

> Effective youth ministry must begin here. To attempt to lead a person spiritually while at the same time neglecting one's own spiritual life would be a travesty. Any leader who fails to take nourishment daily from the Word of God will most certainly degenerate into a voice from a vacuum. It is much too easy and tragically too common to become so busy doing ministry that we forfeit the greatest privilege and most essential priority of all: our own personal walk with God.[4]

In this respect, the Search Committee is wise to investigate whether the candidate is spiritually burned out. A tragic but too common occurrence is that youth ministers who have spiritually exhausted themselves in one ministry look to another in hope of finding spiritual relief.

In a youth workers' survey by Dr. Mark Lamport

of Gordon College, "burnout" was the most frequently cited reason (76 percent of those surveyed) youth leaders would leave their current position of the ministry. Another 26 percent cited "spiritual stagnation," again indicating the potential spiritual costs of youth ministry.[5]

Sadly, the position change seldom provokes the needed revival, and the youth worker either degenerates into Bertolini's "voice from a vacuum" or starts contemplating another move (or even resignation from the ministry).

A survey by Ridge Burns and Pam Campbell indicated that 58 percent of veteran youth workers go through "frequent periods of spiritual dryness."[6] With respect to the candidate's perspective on spiritual health, the Search Committee might want to get his response to a book like *Feeding Your Forgotten Soul*, a book I wrote primarily to identify the causes of burnout in youth pastors.[7] The candidate's responses to this book could help the Search Committee determine the spiritual state as well as the candor with which the candidate faces his spiritual struggles.

**2. A regular (proven) ministry with results.** Woody Phillips writes, "Does the candidate's track record show that he gravitates toward activities, or is he committed to life change? If life change is not his bottom line, then a relational church will not want him."

In terms of youth ministry, the most significant question to ask is, Does this person have a ministry record that demonstrates a love for students? Youth experts Mike Yaconelli and Jim Burns state it succinctly in *High School Ministry*: "Caring about high school kids is the primary prerequisite for working with them. It's that simple."[8]

**3. Self-starter.** On the one hand, the Search Committee wants someone who is self-motivated and does not need a supervisor breathing down her neck to jump-start her into action. On the other hand, the committee does not want an obsessive-compulsive workaholic who will burn herself or her family out in the first thirteen months.

The Search Committee should ask, Is this a person who takes initiative and yet knows how to pace himself? In *Youth Ministry Nuts and Bolts*, Duffy Robbins urges youth ministers to be wise in their management of time. He observes,

> The inexperienced youth worker is often a blur of busyness, always going somewhere and late for the next place, playing catch up and praying that someone will cancel an appointment. Effective youth workers pace their ministries and live balanced lives that allow them to have identities apart from youth work. They have learned to practice disciplines of discernment and alertness.[9]

**4. Spirit of submission, eagerness to learn, and willingness to do whatever is needed to prepare.** How does the Search Committee find out if these qualities exist? Former employers, academic supervisors, and other references are the best sources. What was the candidate's relationship with the previous pastor? Is the previous supervisor on the candidate's list of referrals? If not, why not?

Ability to work with one's supervisor (the senior minister in the case of most youth workers) can determine the long-term success of the candidate. In *The Youth Minister's Survival Guide*, Len Kageler cites the results of a survey of youth pastors who were fired from their jobs. He writes, "Conflict with the senior pastors shoots down many a ministry, and, of those who got fired, it was the most frequent cause (42 percent) listed on my survey."[10]

With these qualities in mind, the Search Committee should give the youth pastor candidate an opportunity early in the face-to-face interview stage to meet with the person who will be the direct supervisor (senior pastor, Christian education director, etc.). This meeting will provide the committee some foundation for asking the candidate, "Would you be willing to work with and learn from the supervisor?" as well as the supervisor, "Do you think the candidate would work well under your supervision?"

**5. Ability to handle money responsibly.** Phillips advises a careful look at the candidate's track record in handling money, both his own and the church's. To illustrate his point, he writes, "I knew a youth pastor who stole money and equipment from his church for a long time." It is a sad fact that leaders in ministry are not immune from such dishonesty. When in doubt, *ask the candidate directly!*

**6. Willingness to work hard.** Phillips asks, "What is the youth ministry candidate's track record on working? Laziness will be a big problem if the person has never learned to work hard." It is easier to help a workaholic relax than it is to light a fire under someone who is lazy.

**7. A cooperative spirit.** No church that desires a youth ministry with growth potential desires a Lone Ranger, so the Search Committee should look for a team player. Does the candidate have experience leading a youth group through a team? Feedback and other references from volunteers at her current church can tell you this.

In the bigger picture, does he know how to work as a member of the total staff team? References from current pastoral coworkers will provide the answer here. A youth worker in one church had tremendous abilities in working with youths, but he insisted that his work was so hard that he had no time for other general pastoral functions such as making hospital visits or leading prayer meetings occasionally. As a result, other members of the church staff resented the youth pastor and the youth ministry.

**8. A growing edge—always learning from books, others, and difficulties.** This quality appears when the candidate answers these questions: "What have you been reading lately to benefit your spiritual pilgrimage?" and "How have you grown and changed over the past three years?"

A youth pastor on the growing edge will determine the difference between a status quo youth ministry and a dynamic, forward-looking youth ministry. But remember again: the youth pastor on the growing edge will work best in a church whose other leaders are on the growing edge. In a stagnant context, the youth pastor with spiritual vitality may be seen as a threat rather than an asset.

**9. A concern for the lost.** Does the candidate enjoy sharing Christ with others? This quality is especially significant to the youth pastor candidate who will be expected to enlarge the scope of the youth ministry outreach. Asking, "How will you seek to reach out to the community?" will usually uncover the heart of the youth worker in this respect.

The Search Committee, realizing that every Christian worker faces the temptation of turning all of her energy to the church at the expense of the nonreligious world, should also ask, "How will you interact with students outside the church who have no apparent spiritual knowledge or hunger?"

Finally, if the candidate has graduated from a Christian high school, a Christian college, and a seminary, the Search Committee should ask, "How much experience do you have actually working with unchurched youths?" A candidate can often theorize about outreach without having actual experience in it.

**10. Acceptance of others, even in disagreement.** Maintaining *unity*—not being divisive or judgmental or legalistic—is especially significant in the church context where the youth pastor will be working with parents. How will she respond to parents who think that her rules are too strict or not strict enough? How will he respond when students criticize their Christian parents for not living as Christians?

The local church is great in its diversity, but pastors who cannot "agree to disagree" will often alienate people and create unnecessary polarization. The Search Committee is not looking for peace at any price but is seeking the ability to communicate acceptance and love to people, even in the face of disagreements.

**11. Very careful in relationships with the opposite sex.** Phillips urges Search Committees to ask, "What is the track record in maintaining sexual purity? If not clean, how has it been dealt with? Is there a lust problem that is not held in check by regular accountability and clearly set boundaries?"

One pastor illustrated how his church learned this lesson the hard way: "We hired a twenty-three-year-old as a ministry assistant in middle school ministry. He became engaged. Within a few weeks of his beginning with us, our youth pastor learned that he was sleeping with his fiancée.

They came to me, and there was no remorse or repentance. They were gone that day. The church cannot tolerate sexual miscues—especially because your young people are watching and forming their own values."

How can the Search Committee find out the answers to these tough questions? One Search Committee asked the candidate bluntly, "Are there any moral skeletons in your closet?" Another used references and asked directly, "What is his pattern of behavior with the opposite sex? Has he maintained a morally high standard?"

This issue gets complicated because the Search Committee can be the agent of God's grace, helping restore a broken person to ministry effectiveness, but restoration through grace occurs best when both parties involved are committed to truthfulness, mercy, forgiveness, and accountability. The challenge facing the Search Committee is determining how to establish this mutual commitment, even during the search process.

**12. Wholeheartedness.** Does the candidate get excited about the challenges she might face in the youth ministry? Does the prefight anticipation of a boxer entering the ring come through as the interview continues? In other words, does the candidate appear to really *want* the job?

The favored spirit of our age is nonchalance. Being radically committed to anything is out of style. Many people see dynamic commitment as an obsessive-compulsive trait, an expression of some type of dysfunctionality.

In contrast, the Christian value is zeal. We who follow our Christian call are expected to do so without reservation and with all the mind, strength, and will. In the early stages, a candidate might be more reserved because of the uncertainty of the progress in the candidating procedure. But as the process continues and a potential youth pastor emerges, excitement and wholehearted enthusiasm should begin to show.

Beware the youth pastor whose career development seems to be the only reason for responding to the Search Committee's interest. A less-skilled person who genuinely wants the challenge of a ministry can often serve more effectively than a multitalented individual who approaches the job with apathy.

## *What to Look for: Ministry Philosophy*

Beyond the personal qualifications, the interview process should highlight the professional qualifications, beginning with the philosophy of ministry. The Search Committee should review chapter 5, "Do We Understand the Philosophy of Church Youth Ministry?" before proceeding to the following questions.

Some of the philosophical questions flow directly out of personal qualities (for example, being a team player). Others relate directly to the Search

Committee's individual context, the principle I call *contextualization*.

**Question 1.** Do the candidate's ministry philosophy and style mesh with those of the church, and especially those of the supervisor? This issue is greater than simply submitting to the person in the supervisory role.

If the church has no evangelism program, an outreach-oriented youth pastor may bring a style of youth ministry that threatens the status quo. The candidate's demonstrated ministry philosophy (which should be demonstrated both in written form and in past experience) needs to be measured against the youth ministry philosophy of the church and of the youth pastor's supervisor— the senior pastor or Christian education director in most churches.

Woody Phillips tells of hiring a youth ministry assistant who was unwilling to adjust to and work alongside the stated ministry philosophy of his superior. The assistant insisted that his way was better. "Better or not was not in question," writes Phillips, "but his ability to submit and work with his boss was."

To identify some of the tensions that might emerge here, see Appendix E, "Testing the Youth Pastor–Senior Pastor Philosophy of Ministry." The Search Committee should ask the youth pastor candidate and the prospective supervisor to respond.

**Question 2.** Is the candidate a team player? The Burns and Campbell survey cited earlier indicated that 65 percent of youth workers felt overwhelmed with job stress.[11] That almost two-thirds of youth workers feel overwhelmed highlights their need to lead the youth group through a team effort.

With this in mind, Jim Tonkowich exhorts Search Committees, "Find someone who can train volunteers.... Look for a team builder rather than a one-man show." Mike Allen of Grace Chapel echoes the same sentiment: "Nobody can do youth ministry alone; volunteers are invaluable. Choose a youth pastor who views support and nurture of volunteers as a priority."

Allen goes on to explain how "in one church, I replaced a youth pastor who was task-oriented and only met with the youth volunteers once per month to review the tasks for the next month. These volunteers did not feel important, nurtured, or supported. They felt used for what they could give. When I came, I began to have Bible studies for the staff and prayer with them. They started to look forward to staff meetings. I fed them so that they could feed the students."

How does the Search Committee uncover a team ministry philosophy like Mike Allen's? Past experience again helps determine this. Consider the style of youth ministry out of which the candidate has come. If the ministry was dedicated to many adults leading through a team, she will most likely reproduce this style.

If, on the other hand, the candidate came out of a

ministry where the youth pastor worked while others watched, he may have unrealistic expectations of himself and an undesirable model of ministry in mind.

**Question 3.** Does the candidate demonstrate enough sensitivity to contextualize his ministry to the church and the culture, or will he stay with methods that worked in a former church assignment?

Our church has imported a number of staff members to the conservative, "cold" Northeast. Some have come from the South, others from the Midwest, and still others from southern California. Several have flourished in our staff leadership while others have floundered. The hinge on which success or failure has swung has been this question of contextualization.

The ones who believed, "New England culture is no different from southern California culture," or "New England culture *is* different, and it's wrong!" have struggled. The ones who asked, "In light of the differences in culture, what ideas or programs from my former ministry can I implement here?" have generally been successful.

**Question 4.** What is the candidate's track record in getting the church's students involved in reaching out to unchurched youths? If this is one of the top expectations of the church and the Search Committee, the candidate ought to articulate a philosophy of outreach and illustrate it through experience.

One church hired a youth pastor to an outreach-oriented position, but conflicts emerged almost immediately. The new youth pastor's goal was to reach out to unchurched youths—with or without the church's youth group members. He was impatient and irritated with "complacent church kids" so he tried to avoid them and dedicate himself to those outside the church.

The church, on the other hand, realized that—despite the commitment to the unchurched—the priority was the youth group members. The goal was for the youth pastor to mobilize them so that they could reach unchurched youths.

The youth pastor behaved as an evangelist; the church wanted someone who could equip and motivate youths to do evangelism themselves.

**Question 5.** What is the candidate's long-term ministry vision? Several questions can demonstrate if she has a long-term vision:

- "What does a young person need to know before graduating from high school?"
- "What are the most important convictions about life you'd like to see instilled in students as a result of your youth ministry?"
- "How do you measure a young person's knowledge and convictions?"

Addressing this long-term view, Burns and Yaconelli write,

Many youth programs do nothing more than wrap the kids in a protective cocoon during high school. These youth programs provide lots of neat friends, great activities, support, advice, fun, counseling, everything except good, solid Christian education that will last. As soon as the high school student graduates, he drops out of the church altogether because he no longer needs a cocoon. A good youth ministry continually challenges high school students to see the implications of their faith in the real world beyond what they know now.[12]

## *What to Look for: Candidate Expectations*

In the interviewing process, the candidate should be allowed and encouraged to voice concerns and questions pertaining to the youth ministry position as well as the church at large. In addition to salary or housing issues, a high-caliber youth pastor candidate will ask questions that the Search Committee must answer honestly. Here are some questions to anticipate:

- "What type of team ministry should I expect with the other members of the pastoral staff? With lay leaders?"
- "What level of discipleship can I expect from the pastor (or my immediate supervisor)?"
- "What type of administrative support will the church provide?"
- "What is the budget for the youth ministry?"

**147**

- "How much will you expect my spouse to be involved in the youth ministry?"

Les Hughey, a veteran in youth ministry now serving at the Scottsdale Bible Church in Scottsdale, Arizona, adds further questions from more experienced youth ministry candidates to the Search Committee:

- "Explain the organizational structure: To whom do I answer? Who represents me before the church boards (elder, deacon, pastor)?"
- "Is there a job description, or do I write one?"
- "How does the staff function (staff meetings, retreats, Bible study and prayer)? Does the staff work hard and play hard?"
- "What is the church's stance on rock music, movies, divorce, and remarriage?"
- "Does the church have a vision for an intern program? For training others in youth ministry leadership?"
- "What will you expect from me regarding children's ministry?"
- "How long do the current staff members expect to stay? Will you give me the freedom to speak to former staff members?"
- "What is the church's view on home-schooling? Christian schools?"
- "Are high school students used in ministry in other areas in the church (children's ministry, for example)?"
- "What is the church's stance on baptism? Communion? Membership?"

- "Do your services have evangelistic invitations?"
- "What would be the reaction if I needed to discipline a teen?"
- "Is youth Sunday school under me or under the Christian education department?"
- "How would you describe the current health of the church?"
- "What is the financial status of the church at large?"
- "What is the current condition of the youth department?"
- "Would I have the freedom to start from scratch, if needed, with the volunteer youth staff?"
- "Are parents expecting a miracle worker?"
- "Is there professional acceptance of a youth pastor as a professional pastor?"
- "What type of audiovisual and/or technological support is available for the youth ministry? Is this equipment specifically for the youth ministry, or is it shared within all of Christian education?"
- "What room or building facilities are available to support the youth ministry? Are these facilities used solely for young people?"
- "If the youth ministry grows, is the church open to hiring a full-time junior high or college-age pastor?"
- "What is the church's long-term plan (one year, five years)?"
- "What about salary and benefits (health-medical, dental, optical; housing; auto; retirement; sabbaticals; vacation; conference time; freedom to do outside ministry; book allowance; continuing education)?"

## *What to Look for: Subjective Issues*

Although an interview process can be quite artificial and may not present a totally fair picture of the candidate, certain subjective observations can be red flags or warnings to the Search Committee.

**Red flag 1: sloppiness.** When a candidate for an intern position in our youth ministry submitted his application handwritten in pencil, I wondered how serious he was about the job.

The Search Committee should consider whether the resume or application form is submitted neatly and adequately completed. Sloppiness might indicate nonchalance about the job or shabbiness in the candidate's overall quality of work.

To get a bigger picture, ask for some copies of handouts that have been produced for previous ministries. If they follow a similar sloppy pattern, the Search Committee can assume that the candidate will produce work of similar quality for the church.

**Red flag 2: self-presentation.** Related to the neatness issue, evaluate how the candidate presents herself. Cleanliness, poise, and dress are all subjective factors, but they may reflect the candidate's self-appraisal as well as the candidate's fit with the church's culture.

One candidate appeared before our elders (who, at that stage in our church's life, were wearing three-piece suits) in jeans and a T-shirt. They admired his obvious willingness to identify with young people, but his appearance made several of the elders question whether he could adjust to other adult groups in the church that would look to him for leadership.

**Red flag 3: tardiness.** Is the candidate perpetually late? Do the forms get returned late? Is he late to meetings? The youth pastor who seems to do everything last minute may reflect a life that is out of control.

**Red flag 4: avoiding the tough issues.** Are there difficult questions that the candidate avoids about past employment? Does she skirt questions related to issues such as disciplining students? Do tough theological questions elicit a nervous response?

Awkwardness in any of these areas should be followed up, usually in the one-on-one context. Perhaps something is being intentionally hidden, and the Search Committee needs to get the answer. Avoidance often reflects a desire to minimize conflict, which may tell the Search Committee that the candidate is either too diplomatic or headed for some major tension in youth work, where confrontation is often necessary.

**Red flag 5: abrasiveness.** Is the candidate excessively negative, dogmatic, or critical in his answers? The Search Committee wants a candidate who is zealous to serve, but the person who responds to every question with the intensity of a revival preacher calling down fire from heaven may reflect that he takes himself too seriously.

The youth pastor who cannot laugh will usually not relate well to students; they desperately need a leader who takes life seriously but himself lightly. This is not to endorse the candidate who laughs at everything. Does she use too much humor? This tendency can be equally abrasive and can keep the Search Committee from understanding the actual convictions of the candidate.

**Red flag 6: insecurity.** How does the candidate relate to authority figures like parents or older pastors? Is there an obvious discomfort? This reaction might indicate a fear of older authorities, which can result later in unhealthy conflicts in the youth ministry.

How does the prospective youth pastor relate to teenagers? Is there an apparent desire to say all the right things so that the teenagers like him? Wanting to be accepted by students may reflect a healthy desire to identify with them, but too much effort to be liked by students may indicate that the candidate will have difficulty in providing strong leadership to them.

All of us are insecure in some ways, but the Search Committee can still ask, Does the candidate appear to have healthy self-knowledge and self-acceptance? Too much nervous laughing or self-denigrating behavior might highlight insecurities that will hamper youth ministry.

On the other hand, excessive piety—which can be an insecure response manifested in a more religious form—can render the youth leader ineffective with teenagers who need to see an example of genuine spirituality.

**Red flag 7: no questions.** In the interview process, does the candidate ask questions about the job reflecting both a desire for the job and a realistic understanding of church work? Has she read up on the church?

Never asking any questions of the Search Committee or the church leaders might reflect *naivete* (the candidate does not know what the job entails so there are no questions), *complacency* (the candidate does not care enough about the job to ask), or *a desperate desire for a job* (the candidate wants the job and does not want to ask anything to jeopardize the opportunity).

Whatever the cause, the Search Committee should dig a little deeper if the candidate never asks questions.

## *Mistakes to Avoid in the Interview Process*

The difficulty of the Search Committee's work can be diminished somewhat by avoiding these extremes in the interviewing process.

**Popularity poll candidating.** If too many youth ministry candidates are presented to the committee simultaneously, the selection process degenerates into a popularity poll that may be won by a person who has the best resume or the most charismatic personality but who might *not* be the best candidate for the youth ministry position.

The best solution is to establish the Youth Pastor Profile, develop a very short list of candidates (two or three at most), and then interview each of them on successive weekends. This procedure enables the Search Committee to process the candidates objectively and allows time to mull over the interviews.

**Hasty promises candidating.** Promising too much too soon, some churches react impulsively to a desirable potential youth pastor.

One church desperately wanted to fill a youth pastor's position before the start of the school year in September. To draw a candidate with a very impressive resume, the Search Committee modified expectations and offered the man far more than the real job would allow him to realize.

When the candidate arrived to start work, promises made in haste returned to haunt the youth pastor and the church.

**Unnecessary roughness candidating.** In contrast to the Search Committee that desperately wants a candidate and will bend over backward to get her, some committees grill the candidate severely. One friend told me of a Search Committee interview where the questions were so hostile, "I felt like they were trying to trap me so that they had a reason to reject me."

Perhaps the committee simply wanted to get the best person, or it was trying to make up for previous failures by other committees. But interviews from a Search Committee with a special agenda can grow harsh. The candidate gets interrogated and leaves thinking, *I wouldn't come to work with such mean people even if they did call me.*

The interviews are most effective when the Search Committee relaxes and understands the essential questions that must be asked for finding the best youth pastor for the church. If the Search Committee believes that the job is to help *both* the church and the candidate discover God's will related to a job fit, the interview process can flow smoothly.

## *The Interview in Review*

Pat MacMillan summarizes,

The interview can be an excellent tool for evaluating a candidate's qualifications, *if:*

- The questions are tied to relevant selection criteria.
- The questions are properly designed to elicit the right information.
- The questions are asked in the suitable manner.
- The climate is conducive to open, candid, nondefensive communication.

- You maintain an attentive, open, nonbiased attitude that allows you to really hear what the candidate is saying.
- You correctly interpret and evaluate the results.[13]

## NOTES

1. Pat MacMillan, *Hiring Excellence* (Colorado Springs: NavPress, 1992), pp. 141–44.

2. Two of the most popular personality/psychological tests include the Myers-Briggs Type Indicator (contact the Center for Applications of Psychological Type, 2720 Northwest Sixth Street, Gainesville, Florida 32609; 800-777-CAPT) and the DISC test (a host of organizations use this method; a recommended contact for the Personal DISCernment Inventory is Team Resources, 5500 Interstate North Parkway, Suite 425, Atlanta, Georgia 30328; 404-956-0985).

3. For information, contact SonLife Ministries, 1119 Wheaton Oaks Court, Wheaton, Illinois 60187.

4. Dewey Bertolini, *Back to the Heart of Youth Work* (Wheaton: Victor Books, 1989), p. 19.

5. Eugene C. Roehlkepartain, ed., *The Youth Ministry Resource Book* (Loveland, Colo.: GROUP Books, 1988), p. 189.

6. Ridge Burns and Pam Campbell, *No Youth Worker Is an Island* (Wheaton: Victor Books, 1992), p. 101.

7. Paul Borthwick, *Feeding Your Forgotten Soul* (Grand Rapids: Zondervan/Youth Specialties, 1990).

8. Mike Yaconelli and Jim Burns, *High School Ministry* (Grand Rapids: Zondervan/Youth Specialties, 1986), p. 94.

9. Duffy Robbins, *Youth Ministry Nuts and Bolts* (Grand Rapids: Zondervan/Youth Specialties, 1990), p. 55.

10. Len Kageler, *The Youth Minister's Survival Guide* (Grand Rapids: Zondervan, 1992), p. 63.

11. Burns and Campbell, *No Youth Worker Is an Island*, p. 101.

12. Yaconelli and Burns, *High School Ministry*, p. 104.

13. MacMillan, *Hiring Excellence*, p. 149.

## Part 6

# The Choice

## Chapter 16

# Making the Choice

**H**ow does the Search Committee finally decide which person to call?

### *Be Prayerful*

Our church has just come through a one-year process of looking for a new senior pastor. In many ways, the situation does not parallel directly a Search Committee's work in looking for a youth pastor, but one theme arose that should undergird any successful search.

We prayed.

When the Search Committee members were chosen, we commissioned them in a church service.

The congregation knelt to pray (an unusual occurrence at our church, reserved only for intense prayer times). As the search continued, people committed themselves to praying daily.

Later in the process, we committed ourselves to a churchwide day of fasting and prayer. At the next meeting, the members of the Search Committee reported unusual unanimity. Several roadblocks that had previously hampered them were removed. They entered the weeks following the day of fasting and prayer with seven people on the short list. They emerged seven weeks later with a unanimous recommendation of one.

Again, we declared a day of fasting and prayer. The elders (our principal decision-making board that would present the candidate to the congregation) entered the phase with many questions. Some were opposed to the candidate. As the night of their vote approached, they appeared divided. If the vote passed, it would be only by the 3-to-1 margin needed.

But they prayed together as the congregation fasted and prayed. They emerged from the meeting with a unanimous endorsement of the candidate. Those who participated called it a miracle!

The point in all this? Search Committees need to do the hard work necessary to investigate candidates, but there is spiritual work that can be done only through prayer. The Search Committee should pray, should recruit others to pray, and should ask the church to fast and pray as the significant and intense choice is made. The future of the church's youth ministry depends on fervent prayer.

In *Hiring Excellence*, consultant Pat MacMillan suggests that prayer is an integral part of the hiring process:

- Pray for wisdom and insight—the ability to discern God's mind, to probe for and understand the gifts and skills of those we evaluate (see 1 Corinthians 2:16; James 1:5).

- Pray for love and wisdom for those we evaluate— that our love will show through and they will feel our acceptance. Pray that they may have insight into God's will for them.

- Pray for courage—to make the right decision for the right reasons. Often the most qualified candidate may not be the most personable, or the person whose strengths most meet our needs may have weaknesses that challenge our "comfort zone."[1]

## *Be Patient*

The Search Committee needs to take the necessary time to make a wise decision. Thorough research, well-reviewed forms, and effective interviews are all part of the process. Talking through and praying about each potential candidate are essential.

The problem for the Search Committee is that the rest of the church might not be patient. Parents want a youth minister *now!* Students complain that 25 percent of their high school experience at church is going by without pastoral leadership. The pressure to act quickly is intense.

Tom McLaughlin advises, "One of the major pitfalls to avoid is hurrying the decision. Be careful not to rush to fill the position. You will expend far more energy in the form of regret or dissatisfaction over a 'mis-fit' locked into the job than you will by taking extra time and making the extra effort."

Steve Macchia advises Search Committees to step back and review each prospective youth worker with three questions.

**1. Character.** Do we like this candidate? He encourages Search Committees to ask, "What are our 'gut' responses to this person?" Although the Search Committee cannot depend solely on instinct, these gut feelings can be either confirmations or hesitations from the Holy Spirit.

**2. Chemistry.** Does the candidate fit this church and staff? A thorough review of the work done earlier in considering the church's culture and the goals for the youth ministry can help assure the Search Committee of a candidate's fit.

**3. Competency.** Is the candidate capable for the challenges of this ministry assignment? Macchia tells of a church whose Search Committee forgot one very basic question: Can the candidate move from a ministry of one size to another that is four times larger? The committee overlooked the com-

# WHAT I LOOK FOR IN A CANDIDATE

In *Hiring Excellence,* Pat MacMillan, who is one of the premier Christian leaders in helping find the right people for the right job, lists twelve character traits he looks for in the best candidates. Many of them stand out as characteristics a Youth Pastor Search Committee should consider:

1. Spiritually mature and growing
2. Emotionally mature
3. Teachable spirit
4. Character (able to "hold the line under fire, make tough decisions, do the right things for the right reasons")
5. Team player
6. Unremitting commitment to excellence
7. Interested in *this* job
8. Cares about people
9. Demonstrated need to achieve ("Is this a person who has demonstrated a consistent ability to set and achieve goals?")
10. Initiative
11. Intelligence ("common sense, judgment, analytical and problem-solving ability")
12. Balance (Is there a "total life pattern of success?")

Taken from Pat MacMillan, *Hiring Excellence* (Colorado Springs: NavPress, 1992), pp. 121–28.

petency requirements for such a jump and later regretted it.

In contrast, the head of another Search Committee used the final choice process as a time to review the committee's stipulations. Before the final interviews took place, he wrote all members a memo that summarized their work and outlined the seven items they had decided were the non-negotiable competency requirements of the church. Such a review took time, but the committee was willing to wait for the best possible candidate.

## *Hire the Best*

Addressing this question of selection, Jim Tonkowich of FOCUS writes, "Hire the best candidate. There is a tendency to find the best candidate and then say, 'Oh, but he won't stay here very long,' and not hire him. First, if you wonder how long the candidate will stay, ask and then *believe what he tells you.*

"Second, even if a youth pastor does not stay forever, someone who does a fantastic job for three years is more valuable than someone who does a mediocre job for ten years. Hire quality."

Elaborating on the issue of anticipated longevity, Tonkowich states, "Don't hold out for the person with a 'lifetime call' to youth work. These people are rare. The nature of the work wears most people out after awhile. . . . Take someone who is ready and willing to serve heartily in this particular call at this particular time. Worry about the next few years, not forever."

## *Be Honest*

One tension regarding a pastoral search is that the Search Committee is working to discern God's call for the church and the leader's life. It is not just an objective process; it involves prayer and the spiritual dimension.

As a result, Search Committee participants may fear expressing their doubts about a candidate. The person who has reservations about someone's ability, character, or giftedness may think, *But how can I criticize this person that everyone else seems to think is God's choice? Who am I to question this servant of God?*

One Search Committee wrote, "Prayer is an essential part of the search process, but it does not eliminate the need for honest discussion, solid research, and hard work. A bozo who has been blessed by a praying Search Committee is still a bozo."

When doubts or reservations arise, speak up. Often one person's questions will be echoed by others who were similarly fearful about speaking up. Honest questions do not nullify a candidate; they ensure that the Search Committee has all of the questions answered *before* recommending a candidate to the congregation.

## *Be Decisive*

Although the decision cannot be rushed, the decision must be made. Prolonging a search in hopes of finding a more perfect candidate often frustrates almost everyone involved in the process.

In one church, the Search Committee hesitated so long that the most qualified candidate withdrew after several months without an answer. He told them, "At first, I really thought this was a match, but the fact that you cannot make up your minds will not keep me from making up mine. Please take my name off your candidate list."

Another youth minister told me of a church that invited him to visit and interview at the church three times before they actually issued him an invitation to become the youth pastor. He asked, "Couldn't they have made up their minds after the first or second visit?"

The process (from initial contact to actual invitation) took almost a year. The candidate got frustrated; the delay created some negative feelings in him when he finally did arrive. The church's young people got frustrated; they waited a full year for a youth pastor they had met several months into the process. The candidate's former church got frustrated, too; his previous board was tempted to release him from ministry simply so that some decision would be made.

## *Present the Candidate*

Every church will differ about how the official decision is made and the invitation issued. In most churches, the Search Committee—after the decision is made—presents the candidate to the ruling board(s), presbytery, or pastor(s). In some churches with a congregational style of government, the ruling board(s) then present the candidate to the congregation for final approval.

Assuming approval by the ruling board(s) and the congregation, the official invitation is made to the candidate by the chairperson of the Search Committee, the Christian education pastor, or the senior minister.

If the candidate accepts the call, one person from the church usually becomes the direct liaison to the new youth pastor. This individual is often the youth pastor's supervisor but could be a member of the Search Committee. Whoever it is, the liaison person must have administrative authority to talk about things like salary start-up, moving expenses, insurance transitions, and the first official day of work. This person, working in conjunction with the Search Committee, is responsible to help the youth pastor through the transition, which will be discussed in the next chapter.

## Contingency Plans

The final choice is made, and the candidate is presented to the necessary boards for final approval, but not every search ends with a candidate receiving a unanimous call from the boards or the church.

We live in an imperfect world and serve in imperfect churches. As a result, we need some contingency plans.

**What do we do if the students reject the candidate?** A friend from a church of two hundred describes how such a disaster occurred at his church: "The Youth Ministry Search Committee felt sure they had found the right prospect, and they brought him in for the standard 'candidate Sunday' (too often a 'rubber-stamp' process); this included a trial run at leading the youth Sunday school class.

"Everyone was all smiles and handshakes with the potential new pastor—that is, everyone but the youths themselves. The congregation voted unanimously to approve him while the youths voted unanimously to reject him. Some youths shared that he never once looked them in the eye while he gave his less-than-inspiring Sunday school lesson. More than a year has passed, and the youths are still less than thrilled about their timid leader."

The writer went on to ask some questions for Search Committees: "How did he get to the point of candidating without a demonstration of speaking and leading abilities? Why were the youths neglected in the approval process?"

His questions offer good insights into how to prevent such a disaster. Make sure that the basic *skills* required for youth ministry have been observed (at the church, at the candidate's former church, or at least by way of video). Also, make sure that *youths are included* sometime before the final decision is made. No church I am aware of will give the youth group veto power over a candidate, but the best churches look for ways to include young people in the process.

**What do we do if the church board or senior pastor rejects the candidate?** If the Search Committee has been communicating regularly with the staff, elders, deacons, and church at large, this should not be a problem. The church leaders will approve the candidate if they have been approving the progress of the Search Committee.

Unusual things do happen in churches, however, so a surprise rejection is not beyond the realm of possibility. Then what?

Realistically, a surprise negative vote may indicate to the Search Committee members that they should resign, making room for a new committee to form and get a fresh start. Someone—either on the staff or on the Search Committee—will need to be put in charge of damage control and communicate the disappointing news to involved parties such as the youths, the volunteer youth staff, and the parents. Appropriate handling of such a surprise vote can avert a church fight or even a split.

The best response would be to consult with the pastor and governing boards to establish a system that would minimize the likelihood of the recurrence of such a surprise decision.

**What do we do if the candidate says no after we have issued the invitation?** This does happen, even though most Search Committees will usually enter a stage with the final candidate assuming that he will accept the invitation if the church votes affirmatively.

Nevertheless, a candidate might change her mind as the Search Committee moves for a final vote. If this refusal occurs, there will be a similar need for damage control, and the Search Committee will need to undertake evaluation:

- Why did the candidate say no? Did we seem to be dragging our feet so that the candidate thought we were indecisive?
- Is the decision reversal an expression of indecisiveness that we would not want in our candidate?
- Since Search Committee members have been through such an intense experience and apparently failed, should we regroup for a second attempt, or should we resign and leave space for a new group who may have more energy to dedicate to the process?

## NOTE

1. Pat MacMillan, *Hiring Excellence* (Colorado Springs: NavPress, 1992), p. 54.

# Part 7

# The Transition

## Chapter 17

# Helping in
# the Transition

**"Y**ou never get a second chance at a first impression." Robert Alias, the media relations expert who served under President Reagan, once stated that a presenter has seven seconds to make the first impression.

The Search Committee now enters into a new phase of its work. The new youth minister has been called; the youth group and the church prepare for the transition. The work of first impressions begins. What are the final responsibilities of the Search Committee?

Mike Allen, high school pastor at Grace Chapel, recently reflected on his third youth ministry move. He compared experiences and offered three categories of transition help: the bare essentials, the positive things a church might do, and the errors to avoid.

## *The Bare Essentials*

**Commitment.** Allen writes, "When you've hired a pastor with certain commitments, do all in your power to keep those commitments. The youth pastor who sees a church committed to him will be committed to that church."

With respect to the economics of the transition, get all the details in writing so as to avoid surprises and unrealized expectations. By explaining clearly, "We pay for this, and you are expected to pay for that," the church can avoid myriad conflicts and disappointments in the earliest days of ministry.

**Transition economics.** Many churches overlook paying for the moving expenses as part of the bare essentials. These expenses should include taking any necessary flights, hiring the moving company, and transporting the automobile(s). Churches often hesitate to absorb these up-front costs because they spend huge amounts of money on a youth pastor who has yet to offer anything to the church.

Paying for these expenses, however, communicates support of and partnership with a youth pastor and family, which can encourage a long and productive ministry time together.

**Housing.** During the move, the Search Committee (or other transition team that the church appoints) can help the youth pastor and family secure adequate housing that is affordable and within reasonable proximity to the church. This step might mean assisting the candidate with a down payment on a home or the security deposit on an apartment. An adequate dwelling is perhaps *the* most significant factor in the transition and adjustment of the youth minister's family.

**Introductions and affirmation.** Early in the transition, someone from the Search Committee should schedule a time for official introductions of the youth pastor to the church at large and the parents of youths. For example, a reception is an opportunity for the church leaders to say, "Here's our new youth pastor. We're proud to say that we've hired the best." This approach is a positive start-up for the new youth ministry.

There should also be a time to meet all of the people with whom the youth pastor will interact professionally: secretaries, custodians, other associates, and relevant committees.

A youth pastor in the Midwest wrote that his transition went smoothly because of his pastor's affirmation. As the pastor introduced the new youth pastor to the adult Bible studies and to the church services, he exclaimed, "We've hired the best youth worker in the state." He offered public praise, opportunities to preach, and visibility in the adult ministry as his way of supporting the new youth pastor.

**Time.** The best gift the church can give a new youth pastor is that of time. Expecting miracles overnight is unfair to both the youth minister and the youths, but well-meaning parents can often communicate high expectations through comments like, "We're looking forward to great things from you."

To offset this pressure, the Search Committee and pastoral leaders of the church should communicate an agreed-upon time frame for the youth pastor to get adjusted. Most new youth leaders will benefit if a church leader communicates, "We are expecting that it will take you two or three months to get adjusted. Take this time to get to know the kids; we're expecting that you will simply maintain the existing program. After two or three months (or earlier if you're ready), let's talk about your dreams and the changes you'd like to make."

One church decided to give the new youth pastor both time and accountability. They assigned the supervisor to work with the youth pastor on goals for year one with a six-month evaluation built in. The youth pastor had direction and a measurable sense of what could realistically be achieved in the first year.

## *Positive Possibilities*

The Search Committee that genuinely wants to help the new youth pastor through the transition can take additional positive steps beyond the bare essentials. These actions can greatly contribute toward making the first year a success.

**Long-distance introductions.** One youth pastor was making the move from the West Coast to the East. He was in his forties and was being called because of his youth ministry expertise. In his own words, "I was coming to this church as their fourth youth worker in four years. I'm not athletic, musical, or handsome. I'm as old as some of the kids' parents. I knew I needed to do something to make a positive first impression."

The incoming youth worker, while he was still living on the West Coast, got the phone number of every student in his soon-to-be youth group. One by one, he called them *before* he arrived. He said, "By calling every one of these students, I was able to communicate that I cared, and this made up for some of the other external weaknesses."

In this case, the youth pastor paid for all of the calls himself, but a Search Committee who really wants the new youth pastor to succeed might want to suggest this idea and then find the money to pay for the calls!

**Cultural guides.** Ridge Burns introduces the idea of cultural guides in *Create in Me a Youth Ministry*. He suggests that several adults be assigned to work alongside the incoming youth worker and family to assist in adaptation to the area.

Burns tells of moving with his wife from the Midwest where "people were very hospitable and had often invited us into their homes." Moving to California, "we felt isolated, unable to build relationships." A cultural guide couple took him and his wife under their wing, listened to their hurts in the transition process, and introduced them around: "Because of their willingness to open their home and their lives to us, we understood more fully why the church, and Californians, functioned the way they did."[1]

Burns suggests that key students serve as similar cultural guides into the youth culture. Two students, Dave and Sue, introduced him to kids, took him to football games, and explained students in the community to him. They built him up in his ability to understand the kids in the church, thus enhancing his success with students and with parents.

**Extra-mile kindness.** Mike Allen adds several other ideas for the church that really wants to support an incoming youth worker:

- Paying for transition fees: new licenses, costs of phone installations, security deposits, or other start-up costs related to settling in a new area
- Filling the cupboards or refrigerator of the new youth pastor's house or apartment with food before the family arrives
- Taking the youth pastor to various stores to give "basic training in local survival skills"

**178**

- Arranging for baby-sitters who can help with children in the transition

**Support through the valley.** A church on the West Coast illustrated positive support in the transition for the incoming youth pastor. The members of the Search Committee agreed when they joined the committee that they would be the new youth pastor's support group for one year. During his first year, the committee met with him every other week, adding support, providing historical perspective, and generally guaranteeing his success.

An ongoing support group for the new youth pastor enables her to go through the inevitable phases of adjustment. Len Kageler calls these the "Morale Curve Trough." "Virtually everyone who goes to a new job," he writes, "cycles through a predictable range of feelings. Some bail out at the bottom, or trough, of the morale curve, just three to six months after arriving." Kageler explains four phases for an incoming youth worker:

- *Phase One:* "The Honeymoon" (usually up to three months). Enthusiasm, optimism, and good feelings predominate. Parents and kids are grateful. Everything looks great; adrenaline is pumping.
- *Phase Two:* "Reality Sets In" (three to six months into the job). Unexpected demands and hidden agendas are revealed. The youth worker sees how far the paycheck *really* goes; feelings of loss or discouragement surface.
- *Phase Three:* "Adjustment Attempts" (six to nine months). The youth worker wonders whether to

**179**

stay at this job, comes to grips with the negatives, and makes decisions about whether there is really a fit.

• *Phase Four:* "Stay and Grow or Exit" (nine to twelve months). The youth pastor decides, Do I stay and try to make a long-term commitment, or do I go to the copy shop with an updated resume?[2]

Ironically, most churches are inclined to give the new youth pastor maximum support throughout the first three months—when she may need it the least! The essential support comes after four or more months: the honeymoon is over, and the youth pastor is deciding whether or not to move on.

Mike Allen emphasizes this point: "Support and *believe in* your youth pastor. Nothing breeds loyalty and hard work more than praise and trust. Youth ministry is difficult ministry. Parents are tense and fearful for their children. Adults want the kids to be quiet. Teenagers want a great program. The youth pastor has to be strong enough to control a mob but soft in heart so that he doesn't explode when he gets hit by a water balloon. Most youth pastors are by nature very giving people who can get very discouraged. They need the leadership of the church to affirm their ministry and encourage them... especially as they are just getting started."

**Build for good supervision.** A youth worker in a parachurch ministry spoke of his difficult transition: "I was a seven-hour drive from my supervisor. Although we had monthly meetings (I took all-night train rides to and from the meetings), I felt so alone in my ministry. There was no one to share my good news or comfort my heartaches. My committee chairman was out of state most of the time, so I had no one but my wife to support and encourage me. That was the lowest period of my youth ministry. I needed supervision—with all of its encouragement and correction—and I received little or none."

That youth worker depicts an extreme scenario in a parachurch ministry, but a similar experience is duplicated in many churches. The new youth pastor arrives, she is shown the basic schedule, and then supervision seems to disappear. She has to learn everything—from how to request checks to how the office machines work—by experience.

The new youth pastor feels alone; a lay leader or even a pastor communicates, "No news is good news, you know," and experience confirms it. He receives feedback only when something goes wrong, parents are upset, or the junior highers make noise in the 11:00 A.M. service.

In contrast, the Search Committee can work to make sure that the youth pastor is welcomed and oriented by the supervisor. The supervisor should be ready to give guidelines for performance reviews, requirements for meetings, and even issues like dress codes for the church office. The new youth pastor will make some mistakes simply because she is new, but supervision can alleviate these errors.

Max DuPree, a Christian business leader, explains the significance of good supervision in any job change. He writes in *Leadership Jazz*, "Clarify how the candidate's performance will be measured. There should be no mystery as to what will constitute acceptable performance and accountability."[3]

## *Errors to Avoid*

**No communication about the program.** The issue of the youth ministry program presents a dilemma to the receiving church. On the one hand, there should not be a preset program firmly entrenched before the new youth minister arrives. An unchangeable program handcuffs the new youth pastor and can cause much frustration in the initial months.

On the other hand, some degree of program and volunteer help must be in place so that the new youth minister does not arrive to a "blank slate" in a church that expects a full program. Specific help in areas like keeping the youth volunteer staff, reserving retreat locations, and securing at least the next quarter of the Sunday school program will be welcomed by most incoming youth workers.

The best way to ensure a smooth transition is to *communicate* during the weeks or months between the call and the arrival of the youth minister. This helps everyone start together with realistic expectations.

**Selective memory.** Promises made in the search process can become great sources of transition tension with the new youth pastor if the Search Committee remembers some of the promises but forgets others.

Youth pastors respond to this issue by identifying certain categories in which Search Committees seemed to forget promises that were verbalized but never written during the interview and invitation process. (Search Committees can avoid these conflicts by listing as many promises and expectations as possible.)

*Exact salary amount.* Several youth workers cited the tension that occurred when the Search Committee communicated the total value of the salary package and the candidate interpreted the package as being the base salary.

*Realm of responsibilities.* "I thought I was being hired as the youth pastor, responsible for junior *and* senior high ministry. Nine months into my job, my supervisor told me I was the high school pastor and changed my job description and my title in one brief conversation," wrote one youth worker.

*Administrative support.* Many youth pastors accept a position thinking that they have a youth secretary. Upon arrival, they find out that the secretary assigned to the youth ministry also serves as the switchboard operator and the secretary to the entire Christian education department.

*Budget support.* One youth pastor commended his Search Committee for the budget they prepared (see Appendix H), but he noticed upon arrival that they had forgotten some basic needs—for example, mailing costs and retreat location deposits. As a result, he felt that the promises of an adequate budget were inaccurate.

*Work expectations.* A youth pastor who had been promised opportunity to preach to the whole congregation found out that he was relegated to the Sunday evening services of three-day weekends. Another had been attracted by promises of two days off per week, but the workload made such a schedule exceptional rather than the average.

**Comparisons to the past.** Avoid repeated references to the "good old days." In a church where a youth pastor is following another who was very successful, there is a temptation to say things like, "We always did it this way with Bob," or "When Bob did this, it was a lot more successful."

Comparison to my successor almost drove me out of our youth ministry here at Grace Chapel. He was a dynamic, musical, humorous, athletic, vivacious person. I saw myself as a steady person, a good teacher, and a strong administrator. We were very different, especially in terms of our first impressions to the students.

Student critique and negative comparison to my predecessor ("you're nowhere near as much fun as ————") hurt me, but the support of the church leaders helped me through the transition. They assured me that I had the gifts and abilities they were looking for.

Such comparison with the past inevitably comes from either parents or youths, but the Search Committee and church leaders can dull the blows by communicating, "You are our choice; change is inevitable; we support your leadership."

## NOTES

1. Ridge Burns with Pam Campbell, *Create in Me a Youth Ministry* (Wheaton: Victor Books, 1986), pp. 42–43.

2. Len Kageler, *The Youth Minister's Survival Guide* (Grand Rapids: Zondervan, 1992), pp. 25–26.

3. Max DuPree, *Leadership Jazz* (New York: Harper and Row, 1992), p. 213.

# *Appendixes*

# The Tools

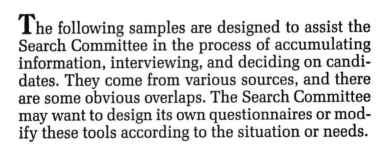

The following samples are designed to assist the Search Committee in the process of accumulating information, interviewing, and deciding on candidates. They come from various sources, and there are some obvious overlaps. The Search Committee may want to design its own questionnaires or modify these tools according to the situation or needs.

## *Appendix A*

# Sample Questions

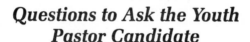

### *Questions to Ask the Youth Pastor Candidate*

Paul Fleischmann suggests the following questions:

1. "Why did you choose to go into youth ministry?"

2. "Picture your ideal discipled student. What are some of the qualities in his life? How would you program to achieve some of these things?"

3. "How would you become an insider at a local high school? Even if you don't know the school, how would you approach it?"

4. "How would you start a youth group from scratch? What might your ministry look like in a year? In three years?"

5. "How would you utilize volunteers, interns, and sponsors? How would you train them?"

6. "How would you integrate your ministry into the life of the church? How would you help to build the whole body?"

7. "What kind of discipleship would you hope for from the pastoral staff and the whole body?"

8. "Tell us about the last person you won to Christ one-on-one. What were the circumstances?"

9. "How does music relate to your philosophy of youth ministry?"

10. "What are some characteristics of your ideal youth ministry situation?"

11. "What three things have you done that have brought you most satisfaction?"

12. "What do you pound the table about? What causes you to weep?"

This list comes from Paul Fleischmann, director of the National Network of Youth Ministries, San Diego, California, used by permission.

## *More Questions for Pulpit Committees and Pastoral Search Teams*

Steven A. Macchia, president of the Evangelistic Association of New England, Burlington, Massachusetts, offers these questions for consideration:

1. Does this person have an ability to bond with a flock/local church and establish good, whole-

some, open, honest relationships and aboveboard communication with the board and staff?

2. Has he been financially provided for in his present ministry, or has that ministry imposed a burden on the pastor and his family?

3. Does he have the ability to affirm other people in their realm of ministry?

4. Does he have a history of doing his own thing, or does he work with a congregation's goals and expectations?

5. What is his level of faithfulness? What areas do you want to check?

6. What is his pattern of obedience? Is he persistent? And a man of endurance? What about his consistency and in what areas?

7. Is he diligent?

8. Is he a man of prayer? Does he pray with his family? Is he really a man of his word?

9. Is he spiritually authentic? For real, genuine?

10. Is there harmony in his home when nobody's watching? Does he promote the role of his wife and her value? Is he a good dad? What would his kids say about him behind his back to the neighbors?

11. Is he a man of moral purity? Ask him!

12. Are his relationships deep or superficial?

13. What is his definition of success in the ministry?

14. What does he feel God honors in the ministry? How do you measure the blessing of God?

15. How does he stem the flow of spiritual pride in his life? How would he address this in a congregation?

16. How does he handle criticism and disappointment? Does he have a group of men presently to whom he is accountable?

17. Is he spiritually resilient? Is he willing to share his struggles with the congregation, or does he have to fight to stay off a pedestal? Does he need the center of attention, or does he crave the credit for ministry success?

18. How does he champion and applaud the quality work of others?

19. What has he done to keep from growing stagnant in his life and ministry?

20. How does he handle the "Monday blues," the normal dips and ups and downs of ministry?

21. How does he cultivate friendships? How does he express his feelings?

22. Does he have a tendency toward workaholism and burnout disease? Does he exercise regularly? What about his diet?

23. How does he involve his spouse with him in ministry, and what are her gifts? Does he realize that his mate is different, and does he value that difference? How does she share her dreams, fears, frustrations, and desires with him?

24. Is he self-absorbed? Does he have to be well-liked?

25. Who are the people who have shaped his values about life and ministry? How?

26. Is he a person of creativity? How does he express it? How does he nourish that creative ability?

27. What does he do when he gets bored and realizes that he has fallen into a rut?

28. How does he provide for healthy evaluation of and honest feedback of his ministry? How does he address any blind spots he might have?

29. How does he expose himself to other viewpoints and vistas in ministry in both style and substance?

## *Questions on Ethics and Theology*

The Search Committee might ask about these basic areas related to personal ethics and theological convictions. Again, church beliefs and tradition should be factored into such a list as well as some of the most challenging issues that the Search Committee perceives are facing the church's youths. A good idea might be to combine this list with the questions offered by Paul Fleischmann (pp. 189–90).

1. Please give us a brief statement on your personal convictions regarding the following:

- Your view of Scripture
- World and life view
- Trinity
- Person and work of Christ
- Justification
- Sanctification
- Baptism
- Gifts of the Holy Spirit
- Evangelism
- Church discipline

2. Tell us about yourself:

- Personal testimony
- Sense of call to ministry
- Your temperament
- Books that have affected you most
- Hobbies

3. Describe your perspectives on and convictions about the following:

- The Christian family
- Smoking
- Use of alcohol
- Abortion
- Rock music
- The media (movies, videos, TV, etc.)
- Pornography
- Dating/teenage sexuality
- Materialism

## *Youth Ministry–Related Questions*

These questions help the Search Committee discern the priorities and philosophy of the youth ministry candidate. They may be best used in an interview context where follow-up questions are possible.

1. "What are your goals and aspirations for youth ministry?"

2. "What is your philosophy of youth ministry as it relates to

- middle school/junior high?"
- high school?"
- college?"

3. "Would you cite two examples of how the Lord has used you to minister effectively to young people?"

4. "What have you found to be the most effective means of developing students as leaders?"

5. "What are your strongest gifts for ministry? Where would you like to see improvement?"

6. "How does your youth ministry strategy pertain to

- Sunday school?"
- youth group meetings and activities?"
- outreach?"
- service projects?"
- work with parents and families?"
- training and using adult volunteers?"

7. "What do you believe to be three of the most critical issues facing young people today? How would you see our ministry responding to these challenges?"

8. "Do you have plans beyond youth ministry, or do you see yourself in youth ministry indefinitely?"

## *Pitfalls in the Interviewing Process*

Pat MacMillan advises interviewers of ten common pitfalls in the interviewing process:

**Pitfall 1: Lack of preparation.** There is no room for winging it.

**Pitfall 2: Poorly constructed questions.** It is especially significant to tie the questions to the selection criteria.

**Pitfall 3: Not taking effective notes.** Do not rely on memory alone! Note taking increases ability to offer objective evaluation.

**Pitfall 4: Talking too much, listening too little.** The Search Committee should say very little.

**Pitfall 5: Not establishing and maintaining rapport with the candidate.** Asking threatening questions at the outset or creating a tense climate deters the candidate from offering candid feedback.

**Pitfall 6: Telegraphing the desired answer.** Beware the temptation to phrase and rephrase questions so as to put answers in someone's mouth.

**Pitfall 7: Taking things at face value.** It is probably safe to assume that candidates will overstate their successes and downplay their failures.

**Pitfall 8: Too much screening, not enough selling.** Do not forget that the Search Committee's attitude and questions can help draw the candidate toward the church; there is no need for an updated version of the Spanish Inquisition.

**Pitfall 9: Jumping to conclusions.** Do not make the hire/no hire decision too quickly.

**Pitfall 10: Stepping over the legal line.** Do not ask questions that break the laws against discrimination.

Taken from Pat MacMillan, *Hiring Excellence* (Colorado Springs: NavPress, 1992), pp. 150–64.

## *Appendix B*

# Ministerial Data Form

This form is adapted from one created by the Presbyterian Church in America; it obviously reflects that tradition. Each Search Committee will need to adapt such a form to reflect the tradition and concerns of its church or denomination.

1. Full name_____ Date completed_____

2. Home address_____ Telephone_____

    City_____ State_____ Zip_____

3. Ordination: Date_____ By_____

4. Current membership_____

5. Education:

Name of institution attended:    Degree_____ Yr. grad._____

    a) College_____

b) Seminary_____

c) Graduate training_____

d) Other professional school_____

e) Special training_____

6. Experience (please list in order since ordination and include month/year; church or field; city/state; presbytery; when begun; when ended):

_____

_____

_____

Other experience—professional, business, or other—that contributes to your use in the ministry:

_____

_____

7. Current position_____

8. Please be specific in answering the following:

a) If you are not now a member of the Presbyterian Church in America, do you intend to support and be active in the denomination?_____

_____

b) Are you in agreement with the system of doctrine, discipline, and government of the Presbyterian Church in America?

☐ Yes     ☐ No     If No, please explain:

_____

_____

9. a) Present pastorate_____ No. of members_____

b) Remuneration:

Yearly cash salary $_____ Manse provided $_____

Annuity fund $_____ Social security $_____

Hospital insurance $_____

Other allowances: Books $_____ Car $_____ Utilities $_____

Other (specify):_____ Vacation _____ weeks

Do these meet your needs? _____

c) Do you operate an automobile in your work?

# Ministerial Data Form

Personal or church owned?_____

10. References: List five to six persons who would be in a position to give an objective evaluation of your training and experience. Include at least three ministers and two laypersons (who are not members of your present church).

_____
Name

_____
Address (Street, City, State, Zip)

_____
Phone (with area code)

_____
Name

_____
Address (Street, City, State, Zip)

_____
Phone (with area code)

_____
Name

_____
Address (Street, City, State, Zip)

_____
Phone (with area code)

_____
Name

_____
Address (Street, City, State, Zip)

_____
Phone (with area code)

_____
Name

_____
Address (Street, City, State, Zip)

_____
Phone (with area code)

## *Appendix C*

# Skill Inventory

In *The Youth Minister's Survival Guide*, Len Kageler asserts that one cause of youth pastors' getting fired from churches was that they were not equipped with the basic skills needed for the job. As a result, he offers two chapters on basic youth ministry management.

The skills he notes provide an excellent checklist against which a Search Committee can ask a candidate to evaluate herself or himself. The Search Committee may also seek the evaluation of a reference on the candidate's resume to compare answers.

### Level One Skills: Working with Kids

1. Interpersonal Skills: ability to develop relationships with students

2. Strong Up-Front Skills: verbal and nonverbal communication skills

3. Administration of Youths: planning, programming, projects, etc.

4. Creativity in Bible Teaching: ability to communicate biblical truth to "sound-bite" listeners

5. Discipleship: able to empower young people to do ministry

## Level Two Skills: Personal Balance and Self-Organization

6. Able to Relax in God's Power: knows how to draw on the power of the Holy Spirit

7. Self-Administration: able to understand the details of ministry and plan to fulfill them

8. Controlling Paper: able to handle paperwork that comes and retrieve paperwork that he/she has created in the past

9. Personal Preparation: able to prepare the necessary lessons for weekly youth ministry

## Level Three Skills: Working Through Adults

10. Visualizing: able to understand what adult volunteers need to do and then write it down in the form of a job description or other list

11. Communication and Follow-Through: able to relate well to adults so that they know what is expected of them

12. Scheduling: plans well enough ahead so that adults can likewise plan for their involvement

13. Motivating: able to mobilize volunteers who are shy by personal example and enthusiasm

14. Time-Frame Expansion: able to do detailed advance planning so as to be at least one step ahead of the volunteers

The list is adapted from Len Kageler, *The Youth Minister's Survival Guide* (Grand Rapids: Zondervan, 1992), pp. 99–119, and is used by permission.

## *Appendix D*

# Job Descriptions

## *Job Description*

Search Committees will want to revise this job description according to their own needs and expectations. It presents a very lofty ideal, but it is designed to highlight the most basic areas of the youth pastor's work.

### I. Overall statement of responsibility
    A. Report to the senior pastor
    B. Oversee the junior high ministry
    C. Pastor and oversee the high school ministry
    D. Serve on the senior staff of the church and contribute to the establishment of strategy, philosophy, and direction of the overall church

### II. Specific duties and responsibilities and weight of each

| HOURS | WEIGHT | RESPONSIBILITIES |
|---|---|---|
| 15 | 25% | Speaking, teaching, and training speakers |
| 1 | 2% | Planning themes and topics and providing focus for drama, media, and music |
| 7 | 12% | Recruiting and training staff |
| 3 | 5% | Administration |
| 2 | 3% | Counseling parents/students |
| 10 | 17% | Discipleship |
| 5 | 8% | Campus ministry/evangelism |
| 3 | 5% | Student leadership training |
| 3 | 5% | Establishing general philosophy and the direction of the ministry—prayer, vision, planning, and evaluation |
| 3 | 5% | Attending camps, retreats, special activities, big events; development of local and world outreach |
| 2.5 | 4% | Working with elders, church staff, and other general church-related work |
| 2.5 | 4% | Junior high ministry |
| 3 | 5% | Continuing education |
| **60** | **100%** | **TOTAL** |

## III. Minimum qualifications
    A. Master's degree
    B. Solid experience
    C. Qualities
        1. Personal qualities: loyal, team man, faithful, available, teachable, persevering, loves students, positive
        2. Spiritual qualities: filled with the Holy Spirit, has established a prayer life and Bible study habits, has a heart for God, meets qualifications of an elder in 1 Timothy 3 and Titus 1

3. Leadership qualifications: people person, good manager, good communicator, visionary, and energetic

This youth minister's job description is excerpted from Ridge Burns and Pam Campbell's *Create in Me a Youth Ministry* (Wheaton: Victor Books, 1986), pp. 48–50, and is used by permission.

## *Job Description 2*

The following job description was written for our youth minister at Grace Chapel, the pastor who oversees junior and senior high ministry in our church. It again presents a lofty ideal, but it reflects the expectations of a Youth Ministry Vision Committee, which evolved into a Youth Pastor Search Committee.

*General Responsibilities*
The Minister of Youth is responsible for all ministries to junior high and senior high students. This includes Sunday school, weekly activities, retreats, outreach, discipleship, and special programs. As a member of the pastoral staff, the Minister of Youth will report directly to the Minister of Christian Education.

*Specific Responsibilities*
1. To recruit, train, and supervise the Director of Junior High Ministries and all lay volunteers serving in Senior High Ministries.

2. To assist the Director of Junior High Ministries in the recruiting and training of lay volunteers who work in the junior high ministry.

3. To provide overall direction, goal setting, uniform strategy, administration, evaluation, and planning for all youth ministries. To coordinate planning with the Minister to Single Adults to ensure continuity of ministry for the graduating seniors.

4. To ensure the continuation of active youth programming, including Sunday school, Youth Evangelism Explosion, regular activities, retreats, music and missions education, service opportunities, summer programs, and specialized leadership training in ministry. To participate actively in the leadership of weekly planning.

5. To provide communication, counsel, and training for the parents of youths. To maintain healthy, caring, discipling relationships with teenagers.

6. To keep alert as to current trends, resources, conferences, and other youth ministries across the country so as to benefit from the innovations and ideas of others in youth ministry.

7. To communicate regularly with the Minister of Christian Education for goal setting, sharing, evaluation, problem solving, and prayer support.

8. To be sensitive to the needs of troubled or hospitalized students and provide adequate care and counsel to the student and his/her family.

9. To communicate regularly with the church family and the Overseeing Elder assigned to youth

ministries regarding the promotion of programs and purposes of the youth ministry.

10. To evaluate, correlate, and approve curriculum to be used in all areas of the youth ministry.

11. To maintain accurate, up-to-date records of all staff and students.

12. To reach out to area campuses with personal evangelism, Bible studies, and programs designed to attract nonbelieving students.

*General Pastoral and Administrative Responsibilities*

1. To serve as the pastor for the lay leaders of the Youth Ministries.

2. To participate in public services as requested.

3. To manage all administrative functions for the youth ministry including long-range planning and budgeting functions.

4. To remain professionally current in one's areas of leadership and ministry, including reading, studying, consulting, training, seminars, and conferences. To make pastoral growth a priority, retreating occasionally for spiritual renewal and refreshment, reading and planning, Bible study, prayer, and fasting.

## *Job Description 3*

The following job description also comes from Grace Chapel, but this one illustrates a youth pastor who has been assigned a very specific ministry with a bigger youth program.

*General Responsibilities*

The Director of Junior High Ministries will be responsible for all ministries related to junior high students at Grace Chapel—including Sunday school, activities, retreats, and summer programs. This person will interface with junior highers, their parents, and a team of youth leaders and will head the ministry as pastor and leader. The time requirement will be about thirty hours per week. The Director of Junior High Ministries will report directly to the Minister of Youth.

*Specific Responsibilities*

*Vision*

1. To assist the Minister of Youth in writing and evaluating long- and short-range goals for the Youth Ministry.

2. To develop and evaluate long- and short-range goals for the Junior High Ministry in accordance with the overall Youth Ministry vision for Grace Chapel junior high students and families as well as those in the community.

*Volunteer Staff*

3. To assist the Minister of Youth in the recruitment of a staff team to work in the Junior High Ministry.

4. To develop the expected responsibilities of volunteer team members. To spend individual time with each team member in interpreting these responsibilities.

5. To be responsible for training, evaluating, and ministering to the team.

*Junior High Ministry*

6. To be the Junior High Ministry team leader, pastoring students, staff, and families associated with the Junior High Ministry.

7. To oversee all ministry and activity programs associated with the Junior High Ministry, specifically: Junior High Sunday school, retreats, activities, summer programs, weekly Bible studies, counseling of students and families.

8. To communicate regularly with the leadership of Pioneer Girls and Christian Service Brigade.

*Qualities Required*

1. Genuine Christian conversion and consistent personal, spiritual growth through prayer, Bible reading, and worship.

2. Acceptance of and adherence to the ARTICLES OF FAITH of Grace Chapel.

3. Sincere desire to bring teenagers to a personal relationship with Jesus Christ and nurture teens in their Christian growth through relational teaching, encouragement, and discipline when necessary.

4. Ability to receive teaching and correction with a Christlike attitude.

# Testing the Youth Pastor–Senior Pastor Philosophy of Ministry

In *The Youth Minister's Survival Guide*, Len Kageler devotes an entire chapter to working positively with your pastor because he knows how vital this relationship is to the success of the youth ministry (as you recall, he notes that a breakdown between pastor and youth pastor was the primary reason listed for the firing of youth pastors—42 percent of the youth workers he studied).

In that chapter, Kageler lists seven statements that a Search Committee might want to use with the youth pastor candidate as well as the senior pastor to test the philosophical agreements and disagreements that they might anticipate.

These statements uncover some of the philosophical foundations on how the church is run and, therefore, how the youth ministry will function as well. For example, if the senior pastor believes that the evangelism flowing from the church should happen haphazardly, a youth pastor who strongly desires a structured evangelism training program for young people will have a very difficult time.

The statements are intended for ratings of "1" (strongly disagree) to "10" (strongly agree). The Search Committee should look for areas of greatest potential conflict, remembering that the youth pastor's philosophy will need to blend with the senior pastor's.

*a)* The church will grow best if it *targets* the population it is trying to reach (baby boomers, for example), instead of consciously trying to reach everyone.

Candidate's score:____     Pastor's score:____

*b)* The pastors should dynamically lead the church, as opposed to hanging back and equipping the people to lead for themselves.

Candidate's score:____     Pastor's score:____

c) The Sunday morning sermon should be aimed at non-Christians primarily, and Christian nurture should take place in a different setting.

Candidate's score:____     Pastor's score:____

*d)* Evangelism should be organized and structured by the church for its people, not just left to happen haphazardly.

Candidate's score:＿＿    Pastor's score:＿＿

*e)* Bible teaching should emphasize practical principles for life. This is much more productive than nebulous teaching about "the Lord working through us."

Candidate's score:＿＿    Pastor's score:＿＿

*f)* The worship service should be like a heavenly party, rather than meditative and reflective.

Candidate's score:＿＿    Pastor's score:＿＿

*g)* The youth pastor and the senior pastor should have a close, supportive friendship.

Candidate's score:＿＿    Pastor's score:＿＿

Kageler exhorts,

All of this is dynamite information—if we are smart enough to figure it out in the candidating process. It is easy to see that if our pastor teaches "the Bible as Principle" and we're starving for the "Christ life," we are in for stomach upset Sunday after Sunday. If we deeply feel the pastor should be the dynamic leader/keeper of the vision, and he sees himself as a laid back facilitator, we're bound to be in conflict.

Taken from Len Kageler, *The Youth Minister's Survival Guide* (Grand Rapids: Zondervan, 1992), pp. 64–65, and used by permission.

## *Appendix F*

# Personal Contacts

In addition to the networks listed in Chapter 14, the following individuals in youth ministry leadership might be willing to help. They train youth workers at the college or seminary level. As a result, they have a great network of new youth workers for Search Committees to consider.

Dr. Dewey Bertolini, The Masters College, 21725 West Placerita Canyon Road, P.O. Box 878, Santa Clarita, California 91322-0878. Phone: 805-259-3540 or 818-367-6193.

Dr. Dean Borgman, Gordon-Conwell Theological Seminary, 133 Essex Street, South Hamilton, Massachusetts 01982. Phone: 508-468-7111.

Dr. Mark Lamport, Gordon College Youth Ministry

Department, Grapevine Road, Wenham, Massachusetts 01984. Phone: 508-927-2300.

Duffy Robbins, Eastern College Youth Ministry Department, St. Davids, Pennsylvania 19087. Phone: 215-341-5959.

Dr. Mark Senter, Trinity Evangelical Divinity School, 2045 Half Day Road, Deerfield, Illinois 60615. Phone: 708-945-8800.

## Appendix G

# Written Resources

Benson, Warren S., and Mark H. Senter III, eds. *The Complete Book of Youth Ministry*. Chicago: Moody Press, 1987.
An overall compendium for youth ministry that might be reviewed as the Search Committee formulates its philosophy of youth ministry.

Dingman, Robert W. *The Search Committee Guidebook for Choosing the Right Leader*. Glendale, CA: Regal, 1989.
A step-by-step guide for matching churches with senior ministers. Some of these ideas will certainly apply to youth workers as well.

MacMillan, Pat. *Hiring Excellence*. Colorado Springs: NavPress, 1992.

A general guide to hiring for any position. Loaded with new insights and parallels from the business world, which churches should consider.

# A Youth Ministry Budget

Every church should have some sort of youth ministry budget established even *before* a youth minister is called. In churches where a former youth minister is being replaced, the existing youth ministry budget might be sufficient, especially since the new youth pastor will usually be placed in leadership in the midst of a fiscal year.

For churches where no youth ministry budget has ever existed, establishing that budget might be the role of the Search Committee. As a result, the Search Committee needs to understand what factors play a part in such a budget.

In addition, establishing a solid youth ministry budget can be one way that a Search Committee can enable the church to indicate the priority of youth ministry even before the new youth pastor is on location.

## The Youth Group Needs Money

I gathered my student leaders together for a vision-and-planning meeting for our youth ministry. I came late and found them in full discussion. They already had several hot ideas cooking: a river-rafting trip, a "super" concert with two or three top Christian musicians, and a gala retreat to Colorado. The room was buzzing with excitement.

As they reviewed their ideas with me, I tried to join in their enthusiasm, but my facial expressions gave away my inner tensions. "What's wrong?" asked one student. "Don't you like our ideas?"

"The ideas are great," I said, "but how much will all this cost? Where's the money going to come from?"

The buzzing stopped. No one had given much thought to money. "We were sorta hoping," muttered one student, "that the church would pay for it."

## Where Will the Money Come From?

The question of cost has flattened creative planning and discouraged many youth groups from starting anything new. Our heightened awareness of expenses and the cost of living, combined with the trends toward decreased giving and a let'stighten-our-belts attitude in churches and organizations, can be discouraging to youth workers.

And no wonder. With Christian concerts costing $10 to $12 per person, retreat weekends at $60 or more per person, and film or video series rentals at a minimum of $75 each, the financial picture for a youth group can be bleak. When the normal costs of youth ministry programs (refreshments, speakers, films, etc.) are combined with extraordinary costs (special functions, emergency needs), the youth leader is left flustered and dismayed. Where *will* the money come from? How much *will* it cost?

Although churches will vary widely in the amount of money available and the methods for allocating funds, an effective youth ministry budget is one of the best possible answers to the financial dilemmas and tensions in the youth program. A thought-through budget is a great gift that a Search Committee can give to a new youth minister.

But how can such a budget be started or improved?

## *Four Budget Questions*

The Search Committee should ask four critical questions to get started on budget planning. The answers to these questions should direct the efforts to be more effective in the budget.

### 1. What is the budget history of the church?
Explore the history of the youth ministry.

*a) What has the youth ministry budget been in the past?* $100? $1,000? Knowing this past amount will help the Search Committee modify dreams and expectations. The committee may be very excited about the newly appointed seminary graduate and her 1,001 new ideas for the youth group, but members may be dismayed after presenting a supporting budget in a church where nothing has been spent in the past on the youth ministry. The response may be, "We are already sticking our necks out by paying for a youth minister, and now you want more money?"

*b) What has the youth budget covered in the past?* Sunday school curricula? Guest speakers? Refreshments? A Youth Pastor Search Committee that discovers the youth budget is $20,000 may get very excited—until the revelation that this amount covers the youth minister's salary, the youth mailings, two retreats, and other ministry-related expenses.

*c) Who controls the youth ministry budget?* An elder? The senior pastor? A parent? The youth minister? When the youth ministry budget is controlled by someone outside the youth ministry (or by someone who has a hidden agenda for the youth ministry), there may be some hidden costs in the budget. If the new youth pastor wants to show a film to the group, does he need to get clearance from the entire board of deacons? Will she find herself wanting to spend money only to have the budget controller tell her that the budget will not cover such an item? Discovering the red tape associated with the budget may not prevent any frustration, but it will at least help the Search Committee prepare the new youth worker for budget-related tensions.

Knowing the history of the youth ministry budget will enable the committee to plan with realistic expectations and awareness of constraints.

**2. When should we begin to plan?** One day in May I received a call from a colleague: "Paul, we're starting to plan our summer program. Do you have any ideas you think could help us?" He was starting to plan for the summer—four weeks before the summer began!

Lack of planning or poor planning hampers many youth ministries in creating summer programs or budgets. A few weeks before Jim's supervisor needed his proposed youth ministry budget for the next year, he reminded himself to set aside some time to think about the budget. Then he got involved in planning the Friday night meeting, and one of the students had a crisis. Then at ten o'clock on the night before the budget was due, Jim remembered he hadn't even begun the final statement. He jotted some figures on a memo pad and handed them in.

The Search Committee cannot afford a similar experience. Some suggestions will help in preparing an upcoming year's budget.

*a) Ask existing volunteers for an ongoing file of needs that should be put into the next year's budget.* The money needed to fix a tire on the August bike trip is hard to remember when establishing the budget in January. Ask the adult volunteers in the youth ministry to write their ideas (or memories of youth ministry expenses), and throw the lists into the file.

*b) Review the budget two or three months before the budget proposal is due.* Use a checklist like this one to review the youth budget:

Does your budget include these items?

_____ Educational resources

_____ Capital equipment (overhead projectors, etc.)

_____ Rental

_____ Purchase

_____ Bus or vehicle rental

_____ Mission trip expenses

_____ Honorariums for speakers/musicians

_____ Film rental

_____ Subsidies or scholarships for retreats

_____ Gifts or prizes

_____ Refreshments

_____ Advertising and youth group mailings

_____ Musical supplies/songbooks

_____ Mileage reimbursement (for leaders who drive)

_____ Decorations or holiday-related supplies

_____ Athletic equipment

_____ Film development for youth group use

_____ Miscellaneous contingency fund

*c) Break down the budget by month.* The treasurer can anticipate cash flow, and the Search Committee can envision a basic outline of the program.

*d) After deciding on the approximate amount of money needed for the next year, prioritize!* It is unrealistic to assume that church leaders will rubber-stamp whatever budget is proposed. If the Budget Review Committee comes back to the Search Committee with a request to cut the budget by 20 percent ("After all, we don't even have a youth pastor yet!"), the Search Committee needs to know the essential and the nonessential items. Prioritizing the budget will enable the Search Committee to make cuts according to anticipated ministry goals, which is much better than having an uninvolved committee cut the budget randomly.

*e) Decide how budgeted monies will be accounted for.* Will a youth group treasurer manage the checking account? Will all money need to go through the church treasurer? Planning ahead for proper management of the fund can save hundreds of headaches later.

**3. What are alternative means of financing?** The financial stresses of our age require that the Search Committee be flexible and innovative in financing youth group activities and needs. Consider these ideas for paying for the program in ways other than a conventional budget.

*a) Let the students pay for themselves.* Statistics show that students on the high school campus today have thirty dollars (or more) per week discretionary spending money. Sadly enough, students are seldom challenged to spend their personal money on service to God or even on fun activities at the church. They spend it on themselves.

Challenging students to pay for themselves doesn't mean they pay for everything, but students should be allowed to "own" their program by being involved financially. When students are responsible to raise their own money for an activity, they have an opportunity to see the power of God at work in people's lives.

Students pay hundreds of their own dollars each year in our youth group for the opportunity to work in a missions setting. When people are astounded that our students *pay* for the chance to *work*, our young people are able to share about how God provided for them in unusual ways. In our materialistic culture, the willingness to spend money in God's work or in His service is one of the greatest expressions of our commitment to live out the lordship of Christ.

*b) Subsidies.* Before draining the church budget of more money, the Search Committee might try to find other people to subsidize student scholarships. The most effective subsidies are gifts from other students. Some young people have jobs that provide them with substantial extra money. A challenge to these students to assist those who have little or no money can enrich the atmosphere of community.

Accepting money from others has its pitfalls, however. First, the person who gives the money may have a hidden agenda for how the money should be used. Parents may give a gift with the hope that their child will get more attention from the new youth leader. Others who subsidize may want some authority in making decisions about the youth group. Even students helping other students can be negative if the givers make the recipients feel guilty or indebted in some way to them.

A second potential pitfall is the effect of the subsidy approach on the youth ministry's reputation. If subsidies are sought too often, people may avoid the youth ministry because they fear that more money will be requested.

*c) Low-cost/no-cost activities.* Marilyn and Dennis Benson's book *Hard Times Catalog* (Loveland, Colo.: GROUP Books, 1982) contains hundreds of ideas for inexpensive youth activities. Realizing that "more people are discovering a lack of 'fat' in budgets and wallets" and noting the increased media conditioning of teenagers to "desire things of the affluent society just as these times are passing away forever," the Bensons offer constructive and creative ways for youth leaders to work toward "zero budgeting."

*d) Youth funding.* In the article "Financing the Youth Program" (*Working with Youth: A Handbook for the Eighties* [Wheaton: Victor Books, 1982]), Leland Hamby suggests that young people can be directly involved in the budget in a way he calls *youth funding.* Through regular offerings taken at their activities and Sunday school classes, students can create their own reserves to be used as needed in the ministry. "The guiding principle behind youth funding," he writes, "is that 50 to 100 percent of all offerings collected in the youth division go into a special youth fund. The remaining percentage, if any, goes into the regular church budget."

Youth funding can be an excellent tool for teaching young people the disciplines of consistent giving and tithing. The only drawback is that if 100 percent of the money collected goes back into youth group expenses, students develop a "giving to ourselves" mentality and are isolated in their giving from the rest of the church body.

*e) Fund-raisers.* Although fund-raisers are usually devoted to needs and projects outside the youth group, sometimes fund-raisers can be used to benefit people within the group. A family in special need, a ministry in which some of the students are involved, and a mission project on which students from the group will serve can be the legitimate recipients of money raised by the group. The leader must be cautious to monitor the use of this money, however, to make sure that fund-raisers don't become an easy way for students to finance activities or things that they should pay for themselves.

*f) Other budgets.* In some church settings, there may be more than one budget out of which the youth ministry can function. Some churches have separate budgets for the Sunday school, for example. Instead of taking money for youth curriculum supplies out of the youth budget, perhaps the Sunday school budget can cover this need. Missions budgets may help in providing scholarships for service projects. Transportation budgets may be the source of money to rent vans or buses for activities and retreats.

**4. Does the budget represent actual needs?** Inexperience in planning a budget can lead the Search Committee to two extremes. On the one hand, it might fail to anticipate all the expenses, and the new youth pastor will arrive, only to find herself out of money five months into a twelve-month budget. To prevent this extreme, the Committee needs to ask these questions to evaluate thoroughness:

*a) Does the budget allow for price increases?* The cost of renting a video or film in April (when the budget is presented) may increase by 10 percent or more by the next February when it is actually rented.

*b) Does the budget reflect the entire ministry?* The Search Committee might be inclined to skew the budget in favor of the ministries in which it is most interested. But overlooking some aspects of the ministry can cause financial and relational tensions.

On the other hand, inexperience makes the Search Committee prey to wish-list budgeting, which lists nonessentials in hopes that the Finance Committee will approve them. The Search Committee can look at the budget this way because a new youth minister is coming and the excitement of a new vision might be building.

Does the youth group *need* video games? Do volunteer staff members *need* to go to Honolulu for training?

The wish-list budget is destructive because it diminishes the credibility and integrity of the youth leader, and it operates as a poor excuse for responsible planning. Remembering that the Search Committee and the forthcoming youth worker are stewards for God's money can help prevent this second extreme.

Responsible budget planning asks, What will the new youth minister and the youth ministry *need* this year to accomplish the church's God-given purposes? The Search Committee must be careful neither to overlook aspects of the ministry that will need financial support nor to disguise "wants" as needs.

## *A Spiritual Perspective on Budgeting*

When stepping into the world of budget planning, the Search Committee may succumb to the temptation to leave behind a spiritual perspective in favor of administrative expertise. But both are needed, and neither should be sacrificed for the other. Three biblical themes will give direction in planning the youth ministry budget.

**Prayer.** God owns everything. Budgets are merely human tools to channel and manage the resources He has entrusted to the church. Use budgets to help the church be responsible in stewardship. Pray for wisdom in establishing the budget. Ask God for the ability to think ahead with vision and thoroughness about financial needs. Trust God to be the supplier of all that is needed.

When budget meetings evolve into fights over minute details on the budget or when the youth group is depressed because the budget got trimmed, the problem is rooted in the attitude toward God. Anger or frustration is at times an indication that the budget planners have forgotten *who* is in charge. Prayer about the budget will keep the Provider in the forefront of the Committee's perspective.

**Integrity.** In light of the dishonesty and greed often associated with organized religion, it is vital to approach the handling of money with a healthy respect. Being above reproach is essential if the Search Committee and the new youth pastor are to glorify God in the use of money.

**Work for the Lord.** It may sound trite, but keeping in mind that God has called members of the Search Committee to support this youth ministry can help in planning an effective budget. That is especially true if members find budgeting to be tiresome or tedious. If reviewed correctly, careful planning of the youth group budget can be seen for what it truly is—an act of obedience to the Lord.

This material is a revision of the article "How To Design an Effective Youth Ministry Budget," which appeared in *Youthworker*, Fall 1984, pp. 22–27.